BEAT ALCOHOL ON YOUR OWN

BEAT ALCOHOL ON YOUR OWN

JON LACKLAND

Copyright © 2022 Jon Lackland

The moral right of the author has been asserted.

Apart from any fair dealing for the purposes of research or private study, or criticism or review, as permitted under the Copyright, Designs and Patents Act 1988, this publication may only be reproduced, stored or transmitted, in any form or by any means, with the prior permission in writing of the publishers, or in the case of reprographic reproduction in accordance with the terms of licences issued by the Copyright Licensing Agency. Enquiries concerning reproduction outside those terms should be sent to the publishers.

Matador
Unit E2 Airfield Business Park,
Harrison Road, Market Harborough,
Leicestershire. LE16 7UL
Tel: 0116 2792299
Email: books@troubador.co.uk
Web: www.troubador.co.uk/matador
Twitter: @matadorbooks

ISBN 978 1803131 092

British Library Cataloguing in Publication Data.
A catalogue record for this book is available from the British Library.

Printed and bound in Great Britain by 4edge Limited
Typeset in 11pt Minion Pro by Troubador Publishing Ltd, Leicester, UK

Matador is an imprint of Troubador Publishing Ltd

Jon Lackland tried many times to give up the drinking that was devastating his career and family relationships, leading him to write this book. In his early forties, having found group therapy couldn't help him and almost at the point of no return, he applied himself to fixing his problem by himself once and for all and devised a completely new strategy to progressively reduce his intake in a safe, controlled manner. He is also now a community champion for alcohol change charities in the UK.

> E-mail: jon.lackland@outlook.com
> Web: www.jonlackland.com
> Twitter: @Jon_Lackland

CONTENTS

To catch a problem	1
Patterns of drinking	17
The strategy of Planned Relapses	40
Tactical Weapons	61
Charting your improvement	106
Changes – the next steps on the path	113
My conclusion – what's yours?	138

CHAPTER ONE

TO CATCH A PROBLEM

Everything said within is true. First, I want to help. It's a real pain when something takes over your being, when a thief takes away your time. Re alcohol I've been there, seen that, got multiple T-shirts from uncountable relapses. I've drunk enough in my time to float an aircraft carrier – aye, and its escorting destroyers as well. I drank like a fish – a Whale Shark to be exact. OK you get the picture – I drank, a lot. I want to share my drink story with you and how I fixed it. If you are sick to the back teeth of booze but constantly battling yourself with it and can't break the cycle read on. We'll develop the strategic and tactical weapons of an arsenal to deploy against this confidence wrecker and then you will actually slow down time – reclaim days that would go by so quickly, alcohol accelerated, then handle the gained time very well. We'll replace the false optimism that drinking gives you with hope for the future grounded on the knowledge that you are working towards it as the best you can be with mind and body unsullied by drink. We'll see that drinking to alleviate boredom is just an excuse that leads to a waste of life. We'll ditch the notion of drink as a coping mechanism (or more accurately a tool to temporarily opt out of life's responsibilities) even in the most uncertain times. And we will answer the question – what replaces the addiction? I understand that addressing a drinking problem isn't easy and realise there is a certain realpolitik involved in it, so we must anticipate, identify and face down all the real temptations that will be placed in our way when we have decided to begin the process of stopping – if we don't, we'll get caught out and fail. There's nothing heroic in self-destruction. We must reduce drink's influence as much as we are able. We will have fun in our programme and measure our progress every step of the way. Our goal is no less than to extend our life spans that have been compromised by alcohol, to have fun living them and to do our duty by ourselves. I've realised the less I drink the luckier I get. So come on then, let's do something lasting! Bacchus be blowed.

Now I'm not going to define alcohol dependence in terms of how many units you drink in a particular period of time or when you drink. You know by your own definition if you have a problem with it. It's finally clicked. You've reached a point where you have accepted the pleasures of booze are outweighed by the downsides. There were many years where in my mind the pleasures at least equalled the downsides, therefore I didn't stop. This isn't to say I shouldn't have stopped, but to me there wasn't a problem caused by alcohol that I couldn't fix by being canny about it – such as papering over any cracks at work with deceit about why I was taking noticeable time off. If Great Aunt Hortense (of the alleged legacy) walked into the room I would be able to become immediately the perfect great nephew even with plenty in me. Once I had accepted the downsides were weighing heavier in the bacchanalian balance though, I had to get it sorted – but sorted by myself. I'll let you into a small secret – I'm a bit introverted and would say ever so slightly sociopathic even (1.9 on a scale of 1-10). In general I like people and like being liked, but was never one to open up too much with personal things to people, except to my family and very close friends and then rarely. I much prefer to sort my problems that are my own business in my own mind. A bit nonconformist nowadays although I suspect I'm not the only one like this. Someone once said, 'know your enemy'. With drink I was my own worst enemy, at constant war with myself. But I also know myself very well. The best person to defeat this enemy was therefore me. So as far as group help for alcohol dependence is concerned, I know it wouldn't have worked with me. I researched such groups and consulted with people who had taken part (with success and failure) and saw actual sessions in action. I admire the work of the individuals who run these groups, as they help lots of people with this addiction who respond to the approach with success. But it wouldn't have worked with me. Group booze quadrilles would have been a pointless dance. Whether this attitude is right or wrong is an incorrect argument – it's a plain fact that it could never have worked with me and I needed a different solution. I imagine in the sessions, if I'd got into the swing of them after declaring I'm an alcoholic, there would have been a short-term cathartic feeling from spilling the beans to the group. I also know that as soon as

I'd got home the session wouldn't amount to a hill of beans for me – if I'd wanted to I would have drank straight away without so much as a by your leave – the approach wouldn't have been sustainable. By taking the sessions I would have merely scorched the snake not killed it. I'm not saying these methods are necessarily flawed and don't wish to appear dismissive because many people have been helped – I'm saying they would not have worked with me. Here's another quite heretical statement – anything that required a hard stop to boozing would never have lasted with me. As a person I grow and change over time as a gradual process. A hard stop is immediate and final, leaving me with no crutch for support and I would fail. Here's another statement that goes against the received wisdom around alcohol dependency – the presence of booze will never totally leave me. But you know I found a way to diminish its presence to mere background radiation by a method of self supporting. I needed a planned, personal process to follow and finally devised one which has worked. And what you do by yourself, accepted totally by you on your own terms and in your own mind – sticks. Also my way is cheap – being from a northern part of the UK I'm especially wary of spending so much as a brass farthing on such a doomed endeavour as booking into a private clinic – plus more on the readmission fees! The clinics are very expensive. Contrast with the fact that at the time of writing you can buy a four pack of 500ml cans of (albeit) German discount supermarket premium lager for £3.39. That's nearly 10 inebriation inducing units meaning you can be at the recommended UK maximum of 14 units per week for a fiver, the price of a half decent cod n chips *without* curry sauce – or if you have to really copper up, in the same store £1.89

buys you 4 cans of 5% cider, so you can be at the maximum for a ludicrous three quid. Have we gone starky? It was ever so in England (ask the falling baby in Hogarth's *Gin Lane*) and other countries, and the cheapness of drink gave rise to temperance movements. I do like the idea of the Temperance Society not least because it had historical roots in the town in which I was born – the term 'teetotal' was first used in a speech by Dickie Turner in Preston, Lancashire in 1833. Its ideals are beyond reproach yet once again I'm concerned that hard stop temperance won't work for everyone. My programme provides tempered temperance which will be more effective for those of us where immediate and full abstinence won't work – and over the long run not many more units will be consumed.

There is yet another truth often recited by the getting off alcohol business that you have to lose everything before you can rebuild and be cured from the 'disease'. There are two problems with this that make it a load of old cobblers. First alcohol may be a very dominant force in your life, but you are also a rational and intelligent homo sapien the rest of the time. Our lives shouldn't be all about just base animal reactions, impulses, needs and wants – you can use your painstakingly evolved intelligence to pull you through. The programme you'll follow makes use of your cleverness to plan the removal of booze and to be prepared for all temptations along the way. You know that the time has come when *HMS You* before long could start its final slide into the icy depths and needs to be stabilised. If you are in a vulnerable state being told you'll lose everything may make it come true, a classic self-fulfilling prophecy, so up front let's pay this thought no heed – any possessions and relationships you have now you will keep and won't lose or degrade them any further due to alcohol. The second problem with this received piece of wisdom is that alcohol dependency is largely an artificial state of mind that can be countered by removing drink from the equation, not a disease to be cured. Chicken pox and Covid are examples of diseases, alcohol dependency is not. It's also not a mental health problem but an addiction imposing enhanced and unnatural feelings on you. Stop the cause of them and they stop. It's a narcotic – it makes you feel good that's its job – to entice you to it time and time again through artificially affecting the balance of certain chemicals within you. To be fair to it, it's upfront about its professed benefits via the TV and in-flight magazine adverts. What it doesn't say on the tin (or bottle) is 'also causes anguish'.

Incidentally, before we start, let's refer to my programme the following of which will ensure your alcohol intake reduces toward zero as 'the path' for want of a better term. We could have called it 'The Mellow Drip Road', 'The Booze Busting Byway', 'The Tipple Termination Turnpike', 'Hammered Halting Highway' or my personal favourite – 'The Cabbaged Cessation Causeway'. Call it what you will to suit you – it's the doing of it not the naming that counts. In this book I'll leave it as the ultra generic 'path'. You can embellish, change or replace this term so you've got it just the way you like it. We need a motto to accompany us on our journey. If we remove the booze goggles what can we not achieve? We'll see unadulterated again without drink's flummery. So our maxim, to be repeated with pride whenever required – 'Mundus in claritate!'

The reason I drank a lot was because I liked it. It made me feel good and relaxed in my own world. This I respectfully suggest is why most drink – to say you drink to escape a family or work problem or to alleviate boredom is to try to provide yourself with a legitimate excuse. On the upward curve of a drinking session any troubles I had were certainly forgotten, but I would not start a session thinking 'right, time to forget my troubles where's the first can?' and at no stage thought anything would be solved. The session started because I badly felt like a drink and the joy it promised. I opted out of real life for a time. The pattern of my drinking was highly personal to me. You will have similar patterns but they will be different in the detail and personal to you. I drank to serious excess mostly alone. I couldn't drink not to get drunk. It was also easy for me not to drink anything – especially when going out when I could watch others drinking without an ounce of craving. What I couldn't do was have a couple of 'social' drinks and call it a day – impossible. If I started drinking I wouldn't stop until I hit the required level of inebriation, and if in a situation with others where this wasn't acceptable for example in the bar entertaining work clients at the end of a working day – well later after I'd left them, even if the venue was in the middle of the Sahara, I would find a way to continue to imbibe to reach the requisite amount one way or another. The reason I drank was because drinking made me feel nice. So nice, that I had a heck of a time opting back in to real life again.

The reason I couldn't stop the drinking cycles, even when I'd convinced myself to hard stop, was because I had no defence against The Trigger. All alcoholics cannot defend against it once it's pulled. Once The Trigger was pulled I had to drink – end of story. Before I formulated this programme there were many consecutive days after a drinking cycle that I didn't drink, but then The Trigger would be pulled again quite out of the blue. It's a switch that hard wired my brain to a state where I had no choice. I am ashamed that I succumbed to it but that is the way it is. When The Trigger is pulled, freewill is scythed down – it operates on a different plane to normal mores. But if you want to free yourself from drink, you must recognise it for what it is and know it. It is the destroyer. One of our major objectives as we embark on the path is to eliminate the conditions The Trigger requires to be pulled – to keep the safety catch on. For this we need stoicism and fortitude aplenty, but no more than we have within us. How ruinous is The Trigger? Well as they say, show don't tell…

One sunny morning a while back I awoke at 06:00 feeling sharp as a tack after a good night's sleep where pleasant dreams had defragged my brain. By the way, I hadn't drunk for ten days and wasn't thinking about drink. Working from home I had my schedule of calls for the day and with confidence was looking forward to it. I took Peggy, our golden retriever, for a walk on the usual route around the country lanes where we live marking the springtime new growth of rosehip and elderberry bushes. Walking back to the house, quite without warning, The Trigger was pulled. I'll have a drink today I thought, it'll be OK – I'll be able to arrange things with work for one day, but tomorrow YOU MUST NOT DRINK, NO WAY, YOU MUST PROMISE ME! I picked up my step and brusquely dumped the dog at the back of the house. I snatched up the car keys and went to the nearest supermarket where I bought three, 4 packs of my regular 5% lager. Returning home, right off I drank my first can – it was 07:30. I then carried on at a rate of about one every 25 minutes. I worked for a large consultancy as a Programme Manager and could do a lot of the work remotely even in those pre Covid days. The first call went well enough at 08:00 – the low amount of lager to that point even made me feel more confident and relieved all restrictions on my brain and thought processes. In subsequent calls, as I drank more, I was unable to concentrate on the facts and figures I had to report to senior teams as the manager of some business critical projects. But I was able to cover to some extent – no-one could guess I was under the influence (who would even consider such a thing at that time in the morning?) After the calls were done I entered a state of pure joy and went outside to drink the next can to immerse myself in nature. I gloried in the rippling life around me and felt I could punch way above myself to the stars – pickled to Picard! But on returning indoors I certainly did no work. About 11:00 someone important e-mailed asking for a call in the early afternoon. I rejected the invite citing a non existing doctor's appointment. Will you stop bugging me I thought? At 12:30 I went to bed and slept for two hours. At 14:45 I went out and bought some more beer because I couldn't face the 16:00 call with the US team without it. I did not perform well on the call. My wife knew when I drank. I would say I could cover four cans from anyone even from her – but of course I never stopped at four. After four she could detect changes in the pitch of my voice and pick up the first hints of fool chattiness. She knew I had been drinking that day. In the evening we rowed – she was scared that the household's only source of income was being jeopardised. Spitting mad, I countered I was perfectly fine and said some nasty things back. I went to bed (as usual on booze cruise days), very early at 20:00 to sleep it all off to be ready for the next day with huge resolve not to drink. That night my mouth was so dry I had to keep coming downstairs for tins of diet coke. In the early hours I awoke with crippling guilt and remorse. I laid awake forensically picking apart all my problems in my mind. I arose and put my gym bag in the car. I drove instead to the supermarket and the previous day repeated itself as did the next. On the fourth I did a horrible cold turkey where I couldn't concentrate on anything. This was the normal cycle of my life. By the way I didn't pass the probation period for that job as I hadn't the previous one. I decided to do something about all this.

The Trigger is a hard-wired state of mind that cannot be reversed once pulled. The more we drink the more likely it is pulled in the days after we try to stop – the smoking gun once fired must find release again. This is because we fail to eliminate the conditions it requires. Feeling badly like a drink and The Trigger are two different things – they operate on different planes. The first is the requirement of a pick me up which drink promises which can be waited out, the second a hard-wired irreversible state of mind. But the first can lead to the second. So we'll develop an arsenal of weapons to eliminate feeling like a drink and the conditions the Trigger requires to be pulled. For each person The Trigger is almost always pulled at a particular time of day – for me the danger time window was from getting up in the morning to 10:00, after this it would hardly ever happen. I may have at times felt badly like a drink after 10:00 but not total compulsion. For others the danger time window will begin at a different time such as immediately after arriving home from work.

Using our arsenal we will stop The Trigger being pulled and alleviate the wanting of a drink at any time.

A central theme in beating alcohol on your own is thorough planning in order to be prepared for every form of temptation that could lead to deviation from the path. During my old drinking cycles, before I embarked on the path, The Trigger used to repeatedly catch me on the hop. Knowing and being ready for it is the key to stopping it. My programme recognises that a hard stop to drinking won't work for very many people. As I've said it certainly didn't work for me – but if I knew I could follow a plan where I could drink just a bit within my efforts to stop, then I would have the opportunity to be my best self. I therefore now introduce the concept of Planned Relapses. If we eliminate the conditions by which The Trigger is pulled and choose the time, location and extent of relapses through thorough planning, we can reduce over time our alcohol consumption by reducing the Planned Relapses. Now we have a practical strategy through which you can beat alcohol on your own.

In my twenties and early thirties I used to smoke a bit, on average about three a day. On Sept 18 2010 I knew that was it, I didn't want to smoke anymore – and from that day to this I haven't. I've often thought why the hard stop approach worked for tobacco and not alcohol. One definite factor was I'd been suckered into thinking that drink enhanced my creativity – whereas tabs only beget more tabs as their sole raison d'être. My main reason for stopping smoking was undoubtedly the inevitable catastrophic health effects. I'd always thought that drinking to excess is bad for you but certainly not on the same scale as cigarettes and therefore I did not forever throw drink over in the same way. I drank in the main lager of 5% abv (any less than 5% was of no use to me and it cut down my range of brands greatly when most reduced to 4.8% a few years ago – couldn't use em). The detrimental health effects of drinking were sort of apparent to me but were definitely not of a magnitude to stop as a cause on their own – it was only beer after all I would think. If you are drinking a bottle of vodka a day they very much should be a reason to cut down drastically as risk of death is if not imminent then certainly on the cards. I actually would drink easily the equivalent of a bottle of spirits a day in beer and did begin to suffer progressively more symptoms of damage – but because the concentration of alcohol was less and taken over a longer period, rightly or wrongly it didn't loom large enough for me as the sole reason to give up. My point is health reasons were a big factor in my wanting to do something about my drinking, but not enough, on their own, for me to stop dead.

I now know the underlying reason why I was unable to stop dead each time I tried was the bleakness of the finality of not being able to have a drink ever again – this caused the conditions for The Trigger to be pulled a few days after deciding to stop – I couldn't really face the prospect. There is a useful analogy to be employed here – another example of where saying never, ever when there is an alternative, a chink of light, often does not work. This is emigration from a homeland. A couple decide they are moving to the destination country for good, half round the world in a cultural or distance sense, utterly sure it is the right thing for them to ensure happiness forever in an economic or beach laden paradise. The happy fortitude built up after the decision has been made is such that the move is carried on a wave of forward-thinking optimism. Then, after some time in the new land, the remembrance of the parents, of siblings and friends, of the smells and sounds, manners and mores of the old country kick in interminably, subconsciously, and one day quite out of the blue, the couple's eyes meet and they decide irrevocably to go home. With drink I was deciding to go home again and again. To move out of this endless cycle I needed to have a safety blanket – to be able to have a drink at some time in the future, but of course to progressively reduce my intake. I say again, this is why those schemes, clinics, programmes etc involving others where you have to stop dead wouldn't work with me. All the mental shoring up imparted by the support of others with alcohol dependence and well-meaning councillors would have dissipated pretty much as soon as I left the building. I needed to reason and plan out my stopping in my own brain. How you stop drinking is complex and highly personal to yourself and only you can really design the elements of your salvation. For some this includes socially interactive help groups – for me it didn't and I venture for many others it won't. When we embark on the path, we will drink again in a planned, controlled and diminishing way. We won't say never again. By doing this we give ourselves the tool of a safety blanket and defer our cravings to a point in the future – the Planned Relapses. This is not a cop out but a practical approach to ensure our drinking reduces toward zero over time. We will use Planned Relapse Days where we drink at a time of our choosing, not The Trigger's, and each relapse will be analysed and lessons will be learnt so the grip and influence of alcohol is progressively relinquished. A programme of Planned Relapses will be followed and an arsenal of weapons developed to counter temptations that will provide the means to ease down on booze and create the conditions where The Trigger's safety catch is left on.

So you have come to the conclusion that the perceived benefits of drink (the initial sense of well-being and joy at the start of a session), are now outweighed by the downsides. You also want to fix it yourself. You have recognised that there exists a trigger within you that when pulled utterly compels you to drink. You also know there are days and weeks at a time where by hook or crook you have created the right conditions where you can stay off it without The Trigger being pulled. But when it is pulled you drink for days and weeks at a time. The patterns of the cycles over time are very similar even if the details of each differ. On each drinking day there is the sense of well-being and joy that is replaced by guilt, self doubt, despair, anguish and all the other associated shit. Sorry for the language but I got so utterly bloody sick of my cycles that had carried on so long, that I had to analyse them and develop a plan to fix them as they were totally messing up my career and relations with my wife. I was constantly at war with myself over drink but knew I had to sort it myself for it to stick. If you have been drinking for a length of time to the extent where you recognise it is a problem then it's always there, the lump of dark matter sitting next to you and following you wherever you go. When you are off it for a couple of weeks say it's still there in a residual form. I like to draw an analogy with gravity. If you are in a space capsule moving away from a planet, the gravity decreases by the inverse square law – so if you move twice the distance away from the planet, its gravitational pull is four times less, four times further one sixteenth less and so on. With drink replace distance with time. The day after stopping drinking the pull of the can/bottle is immense, on day two its grip is much less, day three far less still. As with gravity though there is still always some residual force – a residual pining for booze that it is hard to make go away. For me this residual call of the can meant I needed a process where I could relapse in a safe environment and really analyse what was taking place inside me both physically and mentally and plan for a progressive, sustainable reduction in drink units. But of course models describing life don't exactly follow the tidy rules of the laws of nature. With alcohol addiction there is The Trigger. It is the joker in the pack and can appear at any time if we're not on to it. We must first recognise its existence then think about how we felt when it was pulled in the past – why was it pulled? What weapons can we deploy that will ensure those conditions for its pulling aren't met in the future? The two major forces at work that scuppered my attempts to cut out drink were residual pining and The Trigger. I developed a strategy of Planned Relapses and an arsenal of tactical weapons to deploy in times of imminent danger, to combat both these forces.

Let me say what Planned Relapses are not. A Planned Relapse is not giving yourself leave for a time out to get badgered, an oasis of fun in the giving up desert. At the outset of the process they will be a necessary release of pressure and provide a sturdy staff that allows you, finally, the support and space to succeed in throwing over drink. By planning them and choosing their time and location you are creating a controlled experiment. The first ones you'll be looking forward to hugely. But as you go on you will understand your addiction better at each relapse, really see it for what it is and cut it down to its bare bones – an addiction to a simple molecule called ethanol: six atoms of hydrogen, two of carbon and one of oxygen. The Planned Relapses will reduce towards zero and in themselves become less and less significant, but at the outset they will provide you with a slush fund of will to succeed. Employing Planned Relapses is a strategy in damage limitation, every time you drink there is collateral damage both physical and emotional – but this will now be done under controlled conditions at the time of your choosing and you can use the bad experiences to improve every time. This will lead overall to happy lifetime maximisation as you drink progressively less. I'll show you how to plan and record the events of Planned Relapses a little later.

CHAPTER TWO

PATTERNS OF DRINKING

What is the anatomy of an uncontrolled drinking session? Let's look at one of mine in more detail which took place before I embarked on the path. The reason for this analysis is I want you to cross reference this example of my experience with those of yours and face up to the bad bits of your behaviours when drinking and the anguish you experience afterwards. Then hold a mirror up to yourself and reaffirm the thought that the downsides of drink are now tipping the scales down is indeed the correct one and it is time to do something about it that works. We'll use as an example the boozy workday I've already alluded to. Sometimes on the morn of a working day I would take *An Upon Waking Instantly Contrived Mock Sick Day*. It doesn't matter who you are, how much the ultimate company person you consider yourself to be everyone, but everyone, from time to time wakes up one morning right as rain and thinks sod it I'm not going in – but as a regular drinker with me they happened more often than most. The decision is instant, immediately set in stone and totally irreversible. They are astonishingly spread almost perfectly equidistant throughout the year. Hardly ever on Mondays or Fridays though, to make them appear more genuine and unplanned. On these days, after the awkward and unpleasant task of phoning or more likely e-mailing in with the news followed by the feeling of not quite being believed when the acknowledgement came through from the boss, I would usually drink myself to distraction. I had a free day – now guaranteed hassle free – don't look a gift horse in the mouth! The next morning I would be ravaged by the guilt of what I had done to the greatest degree and have to pick up the pieces of my job whilst dying for a drink and hung over and could have done with a proper sick day. Certain occurrences, Covid for example, can give other opportunities for sick days that no-one will challenge – one for the reaction to the first jab, one for the second and one for the booster. A derivative of this type of day is the invented relative (usually with me from a stock of fave aunts) passing away day. This is how booze subverts you from a good person to one with questionable morals – much of the anguish and guilt is caused by really wanting to be a good person but being unable.

So let's use then as an example of an uncontrolled session that introduced in Chapter 1, a working day sesh that began with The Trigger being pulled that March morning after I had been off drink for a time. OK, strap yourself in, here goes:

The Trigger is pulled at 06:45. Booze needs to be bought from an outlet that has the right stuff i.e. in my case 5% lager (there is a corner shop nearer than the one I go to but it only sells cans that are 4.8% or less). I get home and from the car to the house have already dragged a ring pull back. How do I feel on that first pull? I feel uninhibited joy, that the world is full of possibilities and there are no mental blockages preventing me from exploring them. I sit in front of my computer (remember I am working from home this day) and send off quickly as many e-mails as I can in response to yesterday's issues and those that have sprung up overnight. These are holding messages to show how good I am by responding so rapidly and early in the morning, and to impart the notion I'm working diligently on the problems – got them in hand, just leave me to it. As I feel uninhibited, I actually respond at least as eloquently and effectively than when unimbibed as my brain feels more opened up for this brief period. I am certainly more enthusiastic about the problems than I otherwise would be at this time in the morning. Within the span of four tins, any e-mail appearing in my inbox gets immediately, fully and eloquently responded to. But now I enter a dangerous place. If I was confident I was in a 'safe' work situation – one where I had prepared well say or knew the subject matter that would be discussed inside and out I would decide to be funny after this amount of drink. This is what comes under the heading of *booze induced dangerous courage*. Incidents caused by dangerous courage have contributed to my downfall in more than one job. Here are some examples of my faux (pack) pas:

- In an evening meeting once with members of a customer's firm in an hotel – people who I only knew on a professional basis and then not well. I had drunk a few cans in my hotel room beforehand. The preamble conversation turned to the standard of the hotel gym. I said I was going to visit it the next morning to do some bench presses to address my moobs. I shook my chest in front of the group declaring – 'no harm in a handsome boy showing what he's got!' The silence was 200 decibels. After, my boss took me to one side for a talking to.

- After a few cans one morning (not unlike the one in question) I decided to proactively call the boss to 'touch base' so I could clear out pressing issues he had for me that day in order to continue supping comfortably for its remainder. He was though a stickler for putting calls in the diary beforehand and disliked any off the cuff. Merrily I dialled and he anwered.

    'Can you talk?' I ventured.

    'No, not now,' he replied irritibly.

    'Why – have you had a stroke!?'

    Little did I know that a favourite cousin of his had suffered a fatal stroke only a week earlier.

- Once on an 'all hands call' with all the international personnel from the division of the company I was part of in attendance. The speaker (an IT Director who incidentally ran the women's group which championed equality in the company), was explaining that the firm's e-mail system would be down over the weekend for maintenance, but we could all communicate via our private systems if needs be. I took my phone off mute and loudly blurted – 'then call me Mr Outlook, love, cos I'm a Hot Male!' Not a sound was heard across four continents.

- Sometimes I would accenuate my accent on a call. One friday thinking surely those dialling in from the US, Singapore, France and Italy would instictively know what a Preston accent sounded like and so declare me the king of comedy for adopting it – in response to a question of in which office I had spent the week with the client I replied: 'A went t'Hanover office o'er yon!' One of the senior US directors commented on his difficulty in understanding me to which I declared with raised voice – 'Away thou who heaps aspersions upon my way of talk. Away foul fiend!' The horrified collected shock was palpable. 'He talks in a language of his own divising' should not appear in the appraisal of one wanting to get on in these kinds of organisations (which it did in my next). Not just to the senior people but also to my colleagues, I'd become about as popular as a 'break-out' session at a company training course.

Of course as a manager they don't tell you you're going to get it hot and strong before your quarterly review or appraisal. It happens right there and then and trying to defend yourself is ultimately futile. This was how dangerous courage sank me in jobs that provided us with the means to live.

Anyway, back to the drinking day in question. Another couple of cans take me out of the danger zone because I know now I'm too blitzed to risk direct communication and I go into passive mode, monitoring e-mails and Teams messages only. I'm not so silly to forget the old adage: 'b(ooze)-mail in haste, repent at leisure'. If the phone was to ring I would see who it was on the screen and only reply to the voicemail if it was my boss, only if do or die urgent and only before slapping my face a couple of times and drinking a hyper concentrated black coffee. I set the office communicator to busy. My feelings of joy and possibilities are now at their height. But what do I do? I surf the internet, I watch excerpts from old sitcoms (even those I wouldn't care less about when sober), I check out music videos from exactly the same cadre of songs/artists that I always do in this state – what passion cannot music raise and quell? I look at cars I would like and build up an online profile of them choosing all my personal specs. I'm planning how to deploy the fruits of success not working to attain them. Any work task requiring really detailed thought say designing elements of a complex spreadsheet or a presentation is beyond me now besides which I can't be arsed with it. I go outside to quaff a can and immerse myself in the wonders of nature la la la, ah the exquisiteness of Arcadian wonder! These are real joys there is no doubt about it and they are why I drank. I look up at the sunlit sky and see mares' tails light and airy framed in the deep blue. What a joy their wispy freedom is to behold! But even then something tells me the stratocumulus are soon to come in and cast their mournful piss on my parade. I go back in. If my wife is around I get clandestine, putting my headphones on and participating in faux conference calls – sneaking out from time to time to glug. If not I carry on with my web surfing and occasional e-mail monitoring. If she asks me to do the most basic and reasonable task at this stage such as knocking in a nail or washing up I resent it hugely. But be careful – don't speak too much or she can tell it in your voice (the rise in pitch is now well within her detection sensitivity). At 11:00 thereabouts my imperative is to neck the remaining cans as quickly as possible so my sleep-it-off middayish nap won't begin too late. I put a false meeting in my online diary to cover my sleeping time. I'm hungry so dip into the crappiest of snack choices – crisps, chocolate and a big directly into the tub finger drag of butter. Obviously I'm urinating like a dray horse all this time and get one big one in before setting the alarm for 13:30 and going to bed. I drop off immediately and sleep for ninety minutes. I awake – GUILT! What the hell am I doing? It's a work day! – all the tasks building up that need doing are foremost in my mind. I feel awful because of the crap I ate before sleeping. I check the e-mails. Relief if there are none of any import but if there is something that needs answering (the US people are online now), I get panicky. I swill the porcelain for the umpteenth time that day. Gazing into the bleachy pool made urine cloudy I think bloody hell here we go again. I bite my nails (after washing my hands) and am in a right old state – all my confidence has been dragged out of me and I feel hopelessly vulnerable and open to attack. My head feels reasonably clear but there are still plenty of units in me. There is a video conference call coming up in an hour in which I will have to participate. I can't face it but must. I need some more drink. This time at the supermarket I buy two four packs of small cans of pre-mixed gin and diet tonics (5%) because I don't want any more beer volume. I drink one in the car going home. Leading up to the call I'm nervous and can't prepare. I splash cold water on my face. With seconds to go I suddenly realise that two empty cans are within the laptop camera eye's peripheral vision on the table behind and I quickly knock them off. That would have been proof positive. Zoom and Teams can fatally trip the WFH drinker. Knowing I still look lousy I turn my camera off a second before joining and tell the group I've been having a problem with it which I'll let IT know about. Some must surely mark that this happens quite often with me. I perform not well on the call but not badly enough for immediate recourse from *them*. But the performance I give contributes to the drip drip of a feeling from people that I should be doing a bit better and not be so full of alternate bravado and, well, surliness. After the call I finish the cans not feeling one iota of pleasure from doing so but having no choice – I could not face the hours of the late afternoon otherwise. I put in another false meeting in my calendar. At five o' clock to the second my computer is shut down. If human reactions allowed us to react in fractions of seconds, then I would have shut it down at 17:00 plus one tenth of a second. On some days I would go out again to get three or four more loose pre-mixed gin and diet tonics. I start watching telly as the medium that best occupies my senses so I don't have to think about everything. Now I have a vast and almost insatiable primeval hunger. I eat huge microwaved sandwiches of my own creation – lots of Lancashire cheese, garlic sauce, dripping and turkey ham (an abomination of nature if ever there was one – when aliens come down to see what happened to Humanity there'll be an empty packet of turkey ham fluttering in the breeze). I return to the fridge two or three times – the calories ingested greater in number than the stars on a clear night. Abundant desserts follow. My usual dessert choices are rum baba, sherry trifle, rum and raison ice cream, tipsy cake or tiramisu. Sitting in front of the TV with my wife I try to remain relaxed. But I start having a go at the telly usually something political as she likes to watch the news in the early evening. Or I commandeer the remote and turn over without asking to watch a funny programme. Often I spill some food from my overburdened plate onto my logoed polo shirt she bought me. Whatever the spark an argument is soon raging. The theme is my drinking on a work day, sleeping during the day and the dangers therein. I get really aggressive and pick out anything I can however trivial to fire back at her for example not doing her share of washing up on time and give this equal weighting to the items being thrown against me. I call her some nasty names. She goes upstairs to get away from me. I set myself to watch my programmes, but I'm real tired after eating and I know I need to sleep it all off completely to make up for the day by really knuckling down tomorrow. So I go to bed ridiculously early at 19:30-20:00 sometimes without even cleaning my teeth. I reprise the name calling as I go past our bedroom and the argument flares up again. She says, 'I don't want you anymore like this.' 'What about me urges – am I a capon'? I yell back before smashing the door to the spare room shut. I always by mutual consent sleep in the spare room when drinking. I lie down, put on my ear protectors and actually don't feel in a bad state of mind as I drop off very quickly. I awake at the mid of night with a mouth dryer than the Mariner Valley. I go downstairs quietly – my wife has gone back down to the sitting room. If she hears me an intense, short, vicious reprisal ensues. I drink down a can of diet coke, take one back up and re-enter the room with my attendant Fury. Not much time elapses after becoming horizontal again before the 'Tubal Cains' (in my lexicon of liverishness) start – my heart pounding violently in my chest. The strain on my system feels immense – my heart feels it is beyond its design tolerance. I can't relieve pressure by expunging my poorly designed sandwiches as my digestive system has only just started its grisly work. So I lay awake for a couple of hours, drinking the can then repeatedly going to the bathroom sink to take mouthfuls of water that I scoop up from the tap with my paw. My mental state during the Tubal

Cains is muted because all my thought processes are turned to trying to consciously reduce my heart rate. Sometimes my heart skips a beat and I get bastard scared. But around 02:00 I drop off again as the heart finally slows and becomes less poundy. Savage dreams unhorse my soul. I awake again on the dot as usual at 04:00. As with most people the feeling upon waking is pleasant enough. I have one moment of peace, here at the quiet limit of the world, before it all floods back. GUILT! Before long I start thinking about what I've done and its consequences in two streams – each work problem and the sticking plasters I'm going to have to employ that day and what my wife will do and how I can make it right with her. I know I've been backside slipperingly naughty. Adrenalin rivers begin flowing in my gut. The tides of remorse begin and I start a couple of hours of semi conscious hell, spawned from the knowledge that I'm weeing my life chances up the wall. Writhing under the covers I'm alternately hot and cold – each problem with work appears in turn to torment and I turn each one over not producing any solution in my anxiety – just drowning in a sea of worry, a hippo bag of nerves. The butterflies in my stomach churn into a mish mash of wings and proboscises. My bowels weigh heavily with what used to be carbs, and I expel gas that temporarily works to a lessening effect and my mind is affected more and more, vampiresquely linked to my rectum, and I call the period before I make the first of many trips to the loo to undertake andrexations – Purgatory. I get off the side of the bed, fish for my glasses and head out on the quest to expunge. Expunged, back in bed I am buffeted by the strong winds of lust and take appropriate action. Then the thoughts begin again. What will my wife do this time? Will finally a step be taken to be rid of me? How many more times can I say 'I promise never again' to her? This time I'll make it right. But the overwhelming pressures relate to work. I go over each of the day's upcoming calls again in great detail. I can't go on like this. I'm as far down in the swirling depths as it is possible for me to be without being able to surface. I don't think I could have but in the really worst times, if there was a simple on/off life button to press, there is some percentage of likelihood that I would have pressed it. At 06:30, tired out, I know I must get up. Arise ye more than dead. I sit on the side of the bed all tattered and torn, confused and groggy with a diminishing ringing in my ears as though I was recovering from a blast from a phaser set on stun. Even the simplest upcoming task seems to scare me – the imperative for doing it out of all proportion to its import. So I brood on getting up to clean my teeth a full minute before doing it. Same with all the getting up tasks – more loo visits, shower, getting dressed, taking a massive dose of epsom salts to purge my body and turning on the computer with anxious dread in my breast. The dog pads up – I can't walk her today but do let her out and feed her. I feel horribly distracted as I scan the e-mails that have come in from the US, including those that arrived just after five o' clock UK time the previous evening, which really should have been answered – someone in my role is expected to monitor at least in the evening, this message is even implicit in the content of some of the e-mails wondering why I am not responding. I set the office communicator to busy. You know what though? Now I'm up and have dealt with the most pressing e-mails I don't feel as bad. All I have done though is dampen fires at work – I still have not begun progressing projects. When I do begin a piece of work sharp violins proclaim my jealous pangs, and desperation. The day stretches out before me and with joy I decide I can drink again for just one more day and off I go to the supermarket again. The spiral takes another turn on its downward path. I would usually do four days of drinking in a row obviously getting more into a fix with each day. It was akin to The Big Crunch theory of the Universe. Each day I really tried to fix in my head the awful experiences as they happened, to learn on the job as it were so I had a bank of experience which I could call on to rationalise why I must not drink when the next day dawned. But the laws of the previous day would not survive the night in the same way the natural laws of our universe will not survive the coming together of all matter before the next Big Bang. An appeal from drunk Jon to sober Jon never got through.

If you have a problem with drink you will recognise the pattern I followed and many of the details within it – there's only so many idiosyncrasies within booze addiction. The consequences of it though will differ for each individual. This depends on how you, your loved ones and work associates can handle it and how bad you get when you drink. There are some people, I accept, who can drink each day with no discernable mental side effects. The mental baggage doesn't accompany them. They drink, function more or less OK, have a bit of a bad head the next day – big deal. I was not one of those people and suggest most aren't. It is the guilt spouting from the knowledge that we are screwing up our lives through a damned addiction that makes us feel so very bad. We want to do the best for our family and ourselves to be the best we can be. For me, booze was stopping that and had been for some time, so one day I realised the downsides were outweighing the pleasures and needed to act. I thought about what my wife was going through. I mean what was she supposed to do? She sees me drinking on a work day storing up trouble for our only source of income. She tried to go soflty softly, hand on shoulder but although I appeared to respond it certainly didn't stop me from reoffending. So she got progressively firmer, explaining what was going to happen if I didn't stop in no uncertain terms. In the evening she would be at her wits' end and reiterate all this which I thought of as unnecessarily having a go as I had absolutely planned not to drink the next day. So I would play the whino and whinge about being made to take her tough love. Then I would cross a red line and fire back with whatever cowardly ammunition I could find before going to bed. The next day (if I hadn't thought to take it to bed with me) I often would discover that she had taken and hidden my wallet. The next morning when I was to drink again after all, I would fly into a rage trying to find it but she hid it so well that Sherlock on smack would never have tracked it down. I would wake her and ask where it was, but to her great credit she did not give in. Sometimes there were parking coins in the car – but only enough on average to buy four cans. This was the worst of all possible worlds – I had to stop drinking just as I was getting going and after the fourth can I was faced with the reality of no more stash, of not being able to attain the required level of inebriation – my head was so betwixt and between that I could not function in any capacity. Eventually I would in the day find a way by deception to get more, enough to be sated. I would also always have a job and a half parking. What a bloody life! I knew I shouldn't be drinking but couldn't stop because I was dependant on it. Yet I kept going back to the well and the anger with myself for doing this was tearing me to shreds.

Let's look a bit deeper into my patterns of behaviour within the sorry tale recounted above. If we run through the day again we can try to pick out why I did what I did at each stage. This exercise helped me to design the strategic and tactical weapons of the arsenal that will stop you falling into the same trap over and over and to understand why the trap becomes just as deep each time. In a day's session the only positive aspect at its start was I did as much as possible in a short time in terms of work activities to mitigate the inevitable problems that would arise later because of the session. This is what I term 'drink efficiency'. This is clearing jobs that must be completed and which require higher brain functionality with clinical precision and extreme pace in order to hasten the time to fizzy treats with conscience clear. Drink efficiency prepares the way for the joys to come. You throw yourself into your tasks with gusto, but as we have seen this heightened rate of labour is short lived and other less taxing tanked up pursuits soon take over such as googling the difference between a goblin and a hobgoblin or looking at web sites ranking *Star Trek the Original Series* episodes from best to last – a worthwhile endeavour, no time now to be bored! These internet antics come with their own dangers. Companies can monitor employees' internet activity even when home working with big brother software. If you forget to look at sites just for entertainment value on your home computer and mistakenly do it on the firm's laptop they may well pick it up. A few minutes here and there is OK, but half a day spent on which of the Enterprise, a Star Destroyer, t'Tardis and Battlestar Galactica would win in a scrap may raise a few eyebrows.

The next trait of such a day of drinking is the uninhibited feeling of no mental barriers to overcome allowing you to be creative to write down ideas for an app, a presentation or even a novel – ideas you would never have thought of were it not for the sauce. This is the *fresco* stage of proceedings – painting on a freshly plastered surface. Mostly, however, I remember pen writing or typing lots of inspired stuff and the next day either not being able to read the addled scrawl or not having a clue what I had been on about. But the question has to be asked – what do we perceive is stopping our highest level of uninhibited creativity when stony sober? The answer is nothing – it's about having the confidence that your brain's resources, without recourse to a foreign agent, provides the best outcome.

Deception is a big part of alcohol dependency. So much brain time is devoted to covering up when drunk and sorting out the mess when sober. I was very good at short term boosts of thinking, but bad at the long haul. Unfortunately in the long haul are the frameworks we need for professional success such as building relationships with co-employees, bosses, clients and other *stakeholders* (many of which also have addictions which means you have to put in at least half the effort). These frameworks are far more important in a job than flashes of good ideas – 'it's not what you know, it's who you know' is absolutely true in many business roles. By the way the corporate world, with very few exceptions, is not set up to support alcohol addiction. If it is spotted a way will be found to get the person out, however much lip service the person may receive regarding support on their way out. I was very good at interviews for new jobs – at projecting me and my experiences effectively in a short space of time.

Drink trained deception helped here as I did not exactly lie about why I left old jobs but certainly constructed webs of diversions from the truth – but they came with plenty of associated stress. However, I would usually get a better job than before and start out with all the good intentions of a new beginning. Before long though the beer tap would be turned from drip to trickle to flood and before too long I was having to look around all over again. Using deception as your most trusted skill is no route to happiness and effectiveness in the long haul.

Later on in the drinking day – in my case after the noon nap, guilt first stirred itself. Where booze earlier caused complete inhibition, it now was the cause of complete breakdown in my ability to think with agility as the guilt fuelled anxiety was thrust to the fore. For me this particular type of introspection only occurred when drinking, I never had a tendency to feel this way in periods of sobriety – and often remembered how happy and unfettered by such disability I was when younger before I started institutionalised drinking. Guilt comes on the downward side of the drinking happiness curve. It will always happen every time I drink. It was worse when I knew I definitely should not have been drinking (on a work day say), but is always there to some degree whatever the drinking circumstances. Why? Because even on drinking days where you don't have to get any specific task done – you still know what it's doing to your health, or have the knowledge that you'll be no good for anything the next day if you're going cold turkey, or it's a Sunday and you'll feel lousy on the first day of the working week, or your wife will soon discover you've been drinking and then there will be an argument etc etc – the usual squirts of liquid poo that mean the downsides of drinking under all circumstances are now outweighing the joys. Trying to analyse away the guilt itself is ultimately pointless as we will never get rid of it in the throes of any drinking session. The only way not to experience it is not to drink.

Why did I treat my wife as an outlet for my guilt and frustrations with drink? Even at weekends or on holidays where there was no work repercussions when I drank the day still degenerated into arguments. She wanted me to stop drinking full stop, not just on work days. As I said earlier, I could never drink not to get drunk and she fully understood that whenever I took it up even on a non consequence day I would find ways to become requisitely soused. At first she used to allow me one drink, even two when we went out to dinner but soon learnt that this didn't work and indeed led to disaster. She was trying to find a way to make me stop – with our best intentions central to her. Her methods didn't work with me but the sincerity of her motives and her unhappiness were amongst the very top motives of my deciding to stop. Of course I used to drink with other people and wondered why I behaved differently with them. As an example at least once a year I had a weekend away with four old university friends. As you might expect a lot of pop was necked. I was often the life and soul – acting daft after a few – I certainly never even remotely felt like arguing with them later in the evening. The reason for acting differently with my wife is fairly obvious – my fate was inextricably linked to hers and there was the thing called love involved. I'm skirting around the fact that when she explained in no uncertain terms what was happening to our prospects by drinking I turned into a contrite ultra defensive bully stroke fiend and she was the only person I treated this way. I was now a bad person. With friends though I also turned fiend, it manifested itself differently, more hyper intense joie de vivre/bravado – so in behaving selectively nastily my wife I was now without honour, a coward, a corrupt version of the person I would have been if I had never drunk. I felt myself to be and was in actuality, the brownest of all the bottom wipes, a foulage bar of immense proportion. Carrying on the way I was would have led to her finishing it. She displayed great strength of character in doing battle with a flaky, mega self pitying booze ogre like me. I didn't deserve her but was lucky I had her. Some say, 'you have a problem with drink but don't beat yourself up.' If you are behaving like I was of course you should beat yourself up – give yourself a bloody sound leathering to knock the sense into you to do something. Anyone with half a brain even though it's ale-addled can realise that drink isn't worth it and it's time for an arsenal to be gathered then deployed against it. What if though you haven't got someone else apart yourself to give up for? In other words you're single. I was single for a long period of time before I met my wife. I had exactly the same patterns of drinking in this period as I had when with her before I decided to call it a day and embark on the path. Back then, before my wife came on the scene, I had to travel into work every day so the daily pattern of boozing was different as it started as soon as I could get away from work. The other difference was naturally there was less deception at home because there was just me there. The guilt spats with myself, though, were just as bad and intense – in fact sometimes worse because as I had to go to work hung over, my performance there in person was more obviously poor. Some people are sociable enough to work with others so naturally that even high levels of boozing doesn't take the edge of this aspect of their being effective at work – they are even thought of as good ol' boys and gals because they drink still in some industries. Be it so. With me, however, it was this aspect – the networking, the inviting of colleagues for a spontaneous coffee in the café area to discuss a project outside of the formality of a scheduled meeting, the staying behind at work for the *golf course hours* when many conversations take place in which things really get done and relationships are built leading to promotions that suffered. When I went in, I was surly and avoided human contact as far as possible. If I drank in the evening before a work day I felt I had to exercise at the gym in the morning to give myself some self respect back as much as anything, but also to clear the bodily malaise and sheer mental hang-dogginess I felt – but this meant getting up really early to catch my train and I would get really knackered after a few days. Exercise is a vital weapon in our arsenal as we will see, but as a daily drink recovering agent it is useful only in that it gives the impetus to function to some degree when a working day follows.

So I had the same pressures and desires to quit periodically when single as when I had someone special. The Trigger was activated just the same. Being married and the problems drink was causing my marriage contributed to the realisation that the downsides to drinking were outweighing the pleasures. But I think I would have reached the same conclusion more or less at the same age if single. You stop drinking for others but mostly for you – whether head of a large household, married or single – because if you yourself don't really want to give up, you'll carry on never mind the relatives. Stark reality I know – but this is a nasty business.

Working or unemployed the same tendencies are there. Funnily enough in-between jobs my drinking followed the same basic pattern – the guilt of work tasks building up when drinking when employed, replaced by the guilt of not securing interviews diligently enough. When single the desperate feeling that I would never meet anyone because of the debilitating effect booze was having and the realisation that I wasn't getting any younger was just as powerful as those of guilt following the terrible arguments with my wife. So with a partner or single, working or unemployed – the only way to maximise your happy life span is to do something to make the drinking reduce toward zero.

At this point it's worth discussing cold turkey days. There have been days in your drinking cycle when the night before you've had good intentions to stop the next day but have failed, but in this particular cycle the stopping day has finally arrived and it's time to opt back into life. This with me was because of the accumulation of four consecutive days of misery in body and mind which meant I was all in and it was worth trading one kind of misery for another to secure some sober days and the real happiness they promised. Cold turkey days were usually taken on Fridays which particularly when I was working from home, contained far less onerous tasks and work colleagues were demob happy for the weekend. I hardly ever drank on weekends, which is the opposite of how one might have expected it to go. The quiet mornings without outside pressures meant I looked forward to the two day oasis of seeing the world how it really is without pangs. The Trigger was never pulled on weekends, which shows that it requires a vulnerable mental state or the semi conscious perception that you will need drink to get you through the day. So Fridays were my usual cold turkey days because they weren't demanding and provided a buffer day before the weekend so my mind would be fresh on Saturday so I could apply my mind to any personal project or task unfettered. Contrast this with the feeling of uninhibited creativity at the start of a drinking session. Which is the real deal? I would argue 'Saturday' thinking because drink creativity lasts but the length of three cans after which the mind's output is every greater degrees of gibberish. So let's get back to a working Friday cold turkey day. In the wee (or should I say wee wee) hours of the morning, there is the guilt and anguish that follows any drinking day. Because I'm at the end of a few days drinking the stellar anguish is at its most crippling. Any sound such as the first robin of the morning singing causes me to flinch and produce a gush of adrenalin. Songs that I had listened to on YouTube in the preceding days, whirl in my head in a nonstop shit parade. I drag myself up – once again the simplest tasks loom before me in sequence assuming ridiculous import and imperative – onerous chores to be brooded upon each having to be preceded by a drum roll – clean teeth, drink epsom salts, underpant dressing, each sock application thought about with Jupiter like gravity all in a context of such deep unhappiness and gloom. I don't throw up or even retch though and this is the only cause of feeling proud of myself in the entire day. After making multiple, heroic poonamis, followed by cushellations which join my self belief in the sewer, the day stretches out before me like the M6 with the promised misery of multiple roadworks and reports of obstructions along its length. Once I'm fully up though at least I accept this is a cold turkey day and this shores me up to face the day with some optimism and at the very least ensures I won't drink this day. My concentration is all over the place, 'twixt & 'tween, and I approach every call with deep anxiety – looking at the clock half an hour before it takes place and counting down the minutes. I have no enthusiasm for the job that pays the leccy and mortgage whatsoever. When my wife rises I have four days of compound remorse to impart. I wail 'I can't believe I'm treating you like this, can't believe I'm doing this to myself, I never used to feel this utter sadness all the time, I'm so soooo sorry' – yes I think that about covers the things I used to say to her. My mind won't settle on anything requiring deep reasoning, so I go outside, picking at tasks such as sweeping up the last vestiges of autumn leaves with no great conviction and without completing one job before passing on to another. I just don't know where to put myself. I'm in a frightful funk. I desperately want a drink but don't. A cold turkey day is usually worse on a gloomy day than a sunny one, an overcast day should also have its glories but these are lost in the all pervading introspective dark. As the afternoon creeps on and there is less and less chance of any intrusion from work, at least nothing so important to action immediately, it helps if I do something that gets me out of the house such as visiting the supermarket with my wife. Looking not at the mocking drink aisles I sullenly help her with the lifting and carrying, not bothered at all what food is being selected – eating far from my mind. After arguing with the automated checkout every time it tells me to take the last sodding item out of the bag we return home. It is one hour to 17:00 when I know I'll be home and dry and my outlook will change. The last hour is spent checking the clock as though something actually material will happen at five. When it does arrive it's a relief. I really don't feel like drinking anymore. My glass is no longer bone dry and if not half full at least there is now a sip of hope in it. Why did this happen at this time of day? Why can I face my own time without the buttress of booze but not work? Why was I drinking when I shouldn't, but not now when I in theory could have? I pondered this often and knew the next week I had to change. Over the weekend I had a clear mind, caught up with my exercise regime, never felt like a drink, my wife and I had our usual great time when I was sober. But it was still there, The Trigger, in the background, gun metal gleaming with undiminished brightness. It wasn't long into the following work week or latest the next when it was pulled again.

The experiences just recounted encompass one of my hideous unplanned drink cycles. Do you feel like I did? By understanding the anatomy of the cycles and why I kept to them despite my best efforts to stop, I was able to develop a new strategy and weapons to deploy that would make me get better. Now in the next part of this guide we implement the plan to bring it all to an end. No messing about though – what you are embarking on is a programme that must be followed if you want to throw drink over. We will deal with every tempting agent our minds can conjure that beckon us to deviate from the path. Be of good courage – slowing down time is not something to fear.

CHAPTER THREE

THE STRATEGY OF PLANNED RELAPSES

You have taken the decision that it's time to act upon your problem with alcohol. This may be immediately after a particularly badly ending drinking session, or during a sober period in the cycle. If during a sober period do not be tempted to have one final booze up to 'clear the air' or to 'reset yourself' or to suffer one last time to reinforce and remind yourself why you want to do it. This is the first test of your fortitude. If on the other hand, you have decided immediately after a boozing session then you have to do a cold turkey day. It is perfectly fine if this day is a working day – you have made the decision to do something about alcohol this is the most important thing and you will get though the day and it will be certainly a more successful day than if you drank. It's a far far better thing to have taken the decision and stop than to keep boozing until you reach a day that you think will provide the optimal conditions to stop – such a day doesn't exist. So let's get through the first day directly after the drinking day when you've decided to finally sort yourself out. You've swilled the previous day a lot of depressant, but don't brood on the events of yesterday – focus on the future. Tomorrow you will feel a lot better guaranteed. Today will only be bad if you let it be. Focus on how great things will be. You've taken the first step on the path.

Today you really must not drink. Don't think of taking some kind of 'ease down' day where you might only have half your usual units. They don't work because pound to a penny you'll end up taking the usual number and if you did succeed in having half, the guilt phase would be just as bad as after a full on session and probably much worse as it'll be exacerbated by the knowledge of the failure of falling at the first fence. Don't put yourself through it. Instead summon your fortitude and strength. Physically bring them to the fore as a shield. Encourage yourself and LIKE yourself. Fill yourself with the thought of doing your duty by yourself. Gird yourself for the day ahead. Be happy you have made the decision and let this happiness help you in the determination to do what must be done.

Get through the day. If you need to, put your mind somewhere else. Buy an easy reading magazine such as one of the myriad colourful history titles if that's your thing or a sport magazine – whatever takes your fancy. Flick through the TV menus of channels. Go outside and do some jobs. Don't put pressure on yourself to complete them – the goal today is simply not to drink. No action is too flaky or insincere, no job is too crappily attempted, never mind completed if it means you don't drink. I remember on my first recovery day I did a series of jobs that were half arsed to such a degree it was breathtaking – gutters cleared of less than 40% of their blocking leaves, corn flakes still stuck to supposed washed bowls etc etc – but I didn't drink. By not drinking today you've done a bloody fine A1 job. Play the game for the game's sake today. Be busy not drinking. In dealings with people be civil and courteous but perfunctory is also fine. Basically, keep any opportunity for stresses down to a minimum. Remember it will get better and your level of functionality is about to go through the roof – but for today not to drink is the only objective. Armed with this promise of a brighter future you can even allow yourself to revel in your discomfort as you know that the booze anchor is right now being cut away and *HMS YOU* will be settling onto an even keel.

If you have to go into work on this day after deciding to do something about drinking there will be unavoidable stresses and strains. Keep reminding yourself there won't be a day quite as bad as this again – if you follow the path. Fortune changes as drinking diminishes. Remember no-one's saying you can't drink again – but we are about to set the course to getting your drinking tending towards zero. Isn't this exciting? – why on earth would you want to drink today when you will plan for a life that offers such larks without booze?

The next day you will awake feeling much better and clearer in the head. Exercise becomes very effective to your whole well-being at this time. For me fitness is integral to my whole mind and body performance. Much of my confidence flows from it and it is central to buttressing my edifice of fortitude. When I was drinking and not exercising the downward spirals of both factors fed off and amplified each other. I will deal with fitness and stopping drinking in more detail later, but for now if you are a gym member, like jogging or brisk walking, or anything you can manage – have a really good session today. As terrible as it may initially feel, moving about and working up a sweat is a great way to get your body releasing toxins and you will feel better for it. Also eat healthy today. The stodge and garbage diet I put into my body whilst boozing also spiralled down until it was naught but crisps, chocolate, squeezy cheese and dripping on digestives. When not drinking I had a sensible range of vitamin supplements that I took. These were also defenestrated when on the sauce. So I had an unholy triple helix spiralling down of booze + lessening exercise + poorer food. Eat careful today, nothing too rich. Vitamin C is very effective to feeling better on the day after whether via a supplement or fruit. Fitness and good diet are so very important in the process of getting off booze because they help build a different kind of well-being to the false sort that drink imparts.

Now on this day you need to plan for your first Planned Relapse Day (PRD). Let's get the abbreviations right. From this day forward you will have three types of days. First: Planned Relapse Days (PRD). Second: Recovery Days (RD) – the day immediately following a PRD (the nomenclature 'cold turkey day' is no longer to be used). Third Standard Days (SD) – i.e. every other day. At its highest level our plan is to maximise the number of SDs and ensure PRDs lessen over time and reduce toward zero.

The knowledge of a PRD upcoming will ensure you don't drink in the meantime. At this point you may well think –

hang on I'm off booze why should I want to drink again? But haven't you been here many times before and restarted regular, heavy drink cycles again and again? When the PRD arrives you can defer it – but for now plan for your first ever PRD. Taking PRDs gets us off booze in a controlled and planned way. In moments of weakness in-between them we fix on the next one to get us through. At this point I need to make clear that if you have serious health problems with drink where your doctor has warned you of imminent liver failure for example if you drink ever again this programme of Planned Relapses must not be followed. For others who recognise the point I had reached, we will now look at when to take your first PRD, how to manage the PRD and the outcomes you'll experience and what to do during moments of weakness leading to this first PRD.

I love scuba diving and was a member of the British Sub Aqua Club and will be again. When planning a sojourn underwater I was taught, 'plan the dive, dive the plan' – and this is precisely what you should do for PRDs (or rather 'plan the booze, drink the plan'). I'm sorry to my friends in the diving community for such a horrific corruption of a wonderful rule – but you must not deviate from the plan on the PRD – you will have planned it out to minimise risk to yourself and others. There are red lines you must not cross during the PRD. How you present yourself to the outside world must be controlled and not lead to any trouble. A prime example of a red line is not to drink alcohol before driving, but the planning for the day will ensure this doesn't happen. There are others you can agree with yourself as you know your character after you've had a few. I knew that when under the influence I make best efforts to get under the skin of those who I feel have aggrieved me or slighted me, such as jumping a queue – in order to infuriate them back. I also suffered from flapping gob syndrome – too many verbals on mundane subjects with those I'd just met. So I planned that my social interaction would be minimal after the drinking started.

The first decision to be made when planning you first PRD is when it should be taken. A safe day must be chosen. What do I mean by safe? You must be able to take the day without any prospect of harm to others or your prospects. So this means definitely not a working day or any where you will come into contact or conflict with anyone of any import to you – basically a day where as far as possible you can be on your own and incommunicado. You also cannot take a sick day to undertake a PRD! Think hard about the day you will nominate then ensure your diary will be kept clear on it. Don't choose a day where you expect to hear some important news potentially good or bad – for example the results of a job interview, you don't want any distractions of this type. Don't take a PRD when the next day will be an important work day. If the next day is a work day, make sure it's one where there won't be much to do at least of a stressful nature. What I'm saying is you can't have a voice at the back of your brain reminding you of the trials of tomorrow. You need to be totally at peace on the day. Also don't announce to the world that you are taking a PRD – it won't look particularly good. You are getting this thing fixed on your own – the world will come to know this as your contribution to it comes on big as the bonds of drink are broken. How did I approach my first PRD? I wanted to go through the process totally on my own, planning and analysing each step using my internal resources only. This was really important to me – I had got myself into this mess and would get myself out of it – only I really understand how I tick and would deal with the temptations to come on the path to success. Now I had thought through this programme of PRDs I wanted and needed to carry it out without explaining it to anyone. Some people I knew would have knowingly labelled me as an alcoholic and whatever my improvements they would have continued with the label and used me as a focus to divert from their own deficiencies – if I had made a big song and dance of announcing that I realised what I was and was taking steps to improve. I would recommend you take a similar low key approach with your loved ones – no great fanfare, let your actions do the talking. I wanted my wife to see and experience me getting better and better but how I did it was my thing alone. When she did see me consistently sober, I wanted simply to say I wasn't drinking anymore – nothing more. So which day to choose? Well for PRDs I would always choose a day that would ensure I did not encounter anyone I knew on day itself or the morning after until 0900. So this could be at my house when I knew that my wife would not be there. From time to time she would go to London to visit her old college friend and stayed over for a night or visited family in Germany. These usually happened on a Saturday and this would be the day I would often choose. Plan carefully which day to choose – think through things that might happen to get you busted or interfere with your exile on the day – builders coming round to do some work or a regular visit by a neighbour. If not doing a PRD at home I would plan to go to a hotel for the day. Some expense yes but worth it and a completely controlled environment would be provided. The expense is minimised of course because you will be booking the room some days out and should get a decent price. There is some deceit required here in explaining where you'll be on the day – but worth it and no need to reproach yourself for taking such a decision to check in to a hotel for this purpose. You have to make sure that you are not going to come into any personal contact with anyone who knows you during the day or next early morning. I took the hotel option for my first PRD. A quick word on the type of hotel. A room from one of the many budget chains is ideal – all you're looking for is a clean room in a faceless hotel. Don't go for a cosy B&B – you may be one of a very small number staying there which could lead to some awkward moments – say if the nice couple who run it invite you for a chat in the lounge in the evening when you are five sheets to the wind. One of the big chains is ideal – you want to disappear from society for the day. Another consideration is to make sure you are within easy walking distance of amenities such as takeaways and convenience stores. A red line is you must not drive a car with any alcohol whatsoever inside you. Finally, the hotel should be close to home – no point driving loads of miles to get there and in the case of home emergencies a short taxi ride back only would be required. But situated in the next street where you might barrel into old Mrs Teasdale (with the large grandsons) from number 28 is also not an option. Use your common sense. Anyway I chose a hotel room for my first PRD – it was for a Friday and I took the day off from work. I told my wife I was visiting a client that day at a distance where I could stay over – which I had to do regularly. It was a white lie which undoubtedly any reasonable person would not wish to tell their wife but which had to be done. Don't dwell on this kind of deceit – factor it in as a necessary part of the plan. The overall level of deceit will diminish as does the level of boozing. By planning this first PRD you have made a really important step. You have cancelled your pain through the promise of this day in the future. The bleakness of the finality of never drinking again – the thing that made you restart drinking again and again is no longer yours to experience and despair about. Feel good that you are following a real plan to get yourself off drink in a planned, staged way – know that your drinking henceforth will reduce toward zero.

The day itself goes against the grain of what you may feel giving up looks like. What I mean is you are allowed to booze. If you reach the first PRD and realise that you absolutely do not feel like drinking and have had an easy run since your decision to act you can choose to defer it. If this is the case re-plan the day of your first PRD immediately. The penalty will be if you have booked a hotel on a site that means no refund when cancelling but so what? If you do want to go ahead with your PRD on its original date there is certainly no shame in this. I'll assume you have fixed it so there will be no distractions and you have prepared the ground well. On the day do your usual getting up routine – shower, ablutions etc. If you are using a hotel you won't be able to check in until mid morning at least – this should be taken into account when choosing this type of venue – the check in time may be after your usual first slurp time. Do not buy any drink for the PRD before the day itself. But now on the day, you can go out and buy it. What volume and type? As to volume buy enough so you won't have to think about driving for more if you run out – if you will be further than easy walking distance to a shop that sells it. Be honest with yourself about what this volume is likely to be. You will also be destroying any that's left before you go to bed that night so don't absolutely overdo it and spend too much brass. In terms of alcohol type – buy the type you are used to of the weakest variety that is acceptable to you. For me this was 5% beer or lager, I would not choose 5.2% as I wouldn't choose 4.8%. For my first PRD I bought six, four packs of standard sized cans and ended up destroying two of them at the end. If you drink wine please not bottles of those 14.5% jobs if possible and if it must be spirits water it down to 10% or less i.e. at least four parts water – you are putting your health at an even greater risk by drinking that stuff neat. It all looks rather lurid laid out like this doesn't it – well that's not a bad thing, but you must be sated on a PRD yet keep safe through common sense – we will see how these seemingly two incongruous ideas are reconciled. Before you go out to buy the booze you need to think about the (non drink related) entertainment for the day. For my first one I bought three easy reading magazines of the type I like to read when not much deep thought is wanted. These were two of the history titles you can get nowadays with lots of pictures and colourful diagrams and a light science mag showing the top ten visions of space missions in the next two hundred years. Fun, light but meaty enough to take time over, not just flick throughs. During this first PRD there is no boundary except to try not to drink more units than you would in your past sessions. Do your best to keep to the drinking times you had in your old cycle because you don't want to experiment with new patterns of drinking, this could be dangerous and is not what the PRD is for. For me therefore if taking a PRD at home I would start as soon as I had come back from the supermarket. If in a hotel though I would wait until the earliest I could check in to ensure the red line of drink driving wasn't crossed. The last item of preparation on the day is to plan the food. Whatever you like today – remember though if there are no options for take outs nearby you will need enough victuals to keep you going when the ravenous stage sets in – for me this could mean vast quantities of supermarket sandwiches, nuts, crisps, crap etc. Don't worry too much about nutritional value on PRDs. I wouldn't recommend planning to have a sit down meal at the hotel or any other restaurant with any degree of poshness – you won't cut a suave figure when the sitting time comes! I also wouldn't go on too many walks from a hotel to look at shops, the beach etc (my first PRD was taken on the coast and I had a nice view of the rollers when imbibing commenced) – the reason is you want to lessen a chance meeting with anyone you know or putting yourself in any potential conflict which may be instigated by you because you are intoxicated. Also there's the literal pain of finding loos if you overstretch the walk and can't get back to your room's in time. Of course if you are taking the PRD in your home, you should try not go out into the world full stop. So remember 'plan the booze, drink the plan'. My initial PRD consisted of driving to the hypermarket to buy cans, food and mags then checking into aforesaid hotel to the minute the booking website said was the earliest so to do. In the room I immediately called my wife before the drink would heighten the tone of my voice which she would immediately have picked up with her AWACS strength radar. Luckily she doesn't usually want me making lots of calls for me to see if she's OK when I'm away with work, so my duty to her had been performed. I drank twelve cans right of – first gawping out to sea in an increasingly euphoric state then reading the mags. At about five o' clock I realised I wanted something more than supermarket sandwiches to satisfy my now Roman rapaciousness so after emptying myself thoroughly went to a nearby fish and chip shop for haddock, large chips, saveloy, fishcake and curry sauce. I got back and consumed them in about eighty seconds. Five thousand cals in the day, each one bloody gorgeous. I stood and kicked over a forgotten half full can. I recorded this so to take the volume off the muster of units taken that day as you must – even mulberried, the units taken must be accurately recorded and spillages accounted for. I then slept until 22:00 and awoke still feeling pretty good. I turned on the telly and watched a documentary about Stonehenge drinking all but two of the remaining cans. I finished before midnight as you must – keep to the boundaries of the day. Utterly sated I threw the two cans down the sink, cleaned my teeth, put on my silencing headphones against any naughty shenanigan noises from couples in adjacent rooms, closed my head and went to sleep.

I awoke in the early hours as usual with the usual remorse and guilt. I felt empty and slightly ashamed of the sheer physical amount of the previous day's consumption. I felt this even though it had been anticipated and priced in and I knew that the coming day would not require much in the way of higher brain functions and that there would be no ramifications from my not being able to operate at anything like full capability. But still I felt less than good as what was in my lower digestive system was linked directly to my mood. In fact I felt lousy with a terrible headache and stomach. As I hadn't drank for a while my body wasn't used to such a big drink now and it laid bare all the bad things happening to it. In the old drinking cycles my body was used to it but even though my symptoms were light, the damage was still being done behind the scenes. This is a point your body rams home to you the morning after your first PRD. This time I'll spare you the details of the expunging process. Afterwards back in bed I reminded myself of the first of the three Oaken Rules of PRDs – 'No consecutive drinking days' – they must all be single. At the outset the most important aspect of the process is to get used to drinking on single days only and recover the next day. If you don't do this, you will get yourself back into the old cycle of extended periods of boozing followed by those of abstinence. Therefore we get all the value out of PRDs by keeping them to one day. We look forward to the PRD which ensures our abstinence between PRDs and then learn from its downside. Anyway, now I was into my first Recovery Day. I took my usual hangover remedies. This brings me to another point – don't mix drinks the day before if you don't have to – lessen the upcoming hangover. I think because I only drank beer and kept myself reasonably fit even through all the drinking years I never really got bad hangovers – at least the outward, physical effects were minimised to a point that my wife would not always be able to tell I was drinking the day before due to my appearance, except for the fact that she could pick up that the skin around my eyes looked wrinkly due to dehydration. So before the PRD I'd bought at some little cost an anti-wrinkle face cream which I now applied. I checked out and drove home and said whatever lies I needed to, to her. I knew this was a necessary part of the process. I was truly embarked now on an improvement course that would lead to an immeasurable improvement in happiness for both of us. On the first Recovery Day you need to give yourself time to reflect on where you are in the process, why you are doing it and the benefits it will bring and where attempts at getting better have gone wrong in the past. This day will be tough. I remember I badly wanted a drink up to 17:00 when the feeling totally went away. I would have gone to the gym for a hard workout but in the previous two years I had found that if I exercised the day after a drinking session I would be prone to the bits of me which had undergone exercise swelling up. If you are really desperate the next chapter will detail the elements of a tactical armoury which can be deployed to counter any temptations. It is important to keep a diary of the number of units taken during the PRDs – this is integral to recording your progress and improvement. For me my cans handily displayed their content of 2.2 units. If you took watered down spirits the calculation may be slightly more complicated but must be carried out with honesty and each time the method of calculation must be consistent. The day of the next PRD must be planned on the RD or the day after (i.e. the first SD). If you are suffering on the RD it can be useful to do it then so you have immediately something to look forward to and take the pain away. In planning your second PRD there is another Oaken Rule to take into account – 'the time to next PRD must be longer than the period leading to the preceding one'. Oh and by the way it is written that the time to the next one must be at least 24 hours longer than it was to the preceding one – no trying one hour longer! There is some clarification of this rule required for your first two PRDs. The date of your first PRD is considered to be day 1 of following the programme, not the date you planned your first PRD. This means the earliest you can take your second PRD is two days after the first. Back to my first RD – I was pleased I had just completed my first PRD but knew one wagtail doesn't make a winter so I planned my second PRD early on in the day. After we have completed a PRD we want to plan the next only. This is because we re-evaluate and adjust how we feel about alcohol after each one. It's impossible to plan the one after that because we don't know precisely how we will feel after the next. We may be ready to put in a significant delay. This is the third and final Oaken Rule of PRDs – 'Plan one PRD at a time'.

On the next day (i.e. my first ever SD) I awoke feeling really good and since a long time, without fear. I felt I would never need another PRD again but kept the one planned in the diary anyway. The next suitable safe day I had planned was ten days hence. I told myself I could defer it if I reached the day without any need. Be careful in the planning for the next PRD. The criterion according to the Second Oaken Rule is it must be further away than the time leading to the previous one – and of course on a safe day. Only concentrate on the next one. All I want from you is a planned reduction over time that follows the Oaken Rules. I went to the gym that first SD and as I did my thing I began to really reflect on the events of the first PRD. The euphoria was there yes when I was drinking. I wanted to be aware on subsequent PRDs of the artificialness of the inducement of the euphoria, that it's just euphoria for euphoria's sake, smoke without fire. I wanted to better my life with strong lasting roots. I thought I want to use every scrap of intelligence and sober creativity I have to be the best I can be not helped along by the charlatan and ultimately useless effects of booze. I may not be Brain of Britain, I can't change my genes, but I can be true to myself (and my mum and dad) by wringing out the maximum of what I do have. In the next PRD I wanted to think of this as the euphoria crept over me. Sometimes, when you analyse a 'fun' action at the time you are doing it, all the fun and spontaneity is taken from it, and during the next PRD this is what I planned to do with the boozing session so I could really see the false fun for what it is and in so doing it would turn to dust. Drunk Jon might at last get through to sober Jon.

So soon after the first PRD we have to be aware that there are unexpected dangers around and we must be prepared for them before they strike. By being aware that they are out there we can be ready for them and construct weapons against them. I'll give you an example that struck me during my first SD. My wife had bought a horse a couple of months previously. *Trigger*, she unknowingly named it – laugh? I nearly cashed in my Nectar points! One of my jobs was to go to the stable to give it an early morning feed, which I did after I returned from the gym. There being no decent grass to graze yet she was on bags of horse haylage. The fermentation process in producing it makes it smell like a brewery. Say no more – on cutting open a bag and catching a whiff I had a big pang. I gave myself a few moments and waited it out. If I hadn't already planned the day of my second PRD, The Trigger may well have been pulled. I would spare you the shock of similar occurrences – there are dangers out there and you won't know what they are before they arise. As Churchill said, 'allowance must be made for the intervention of the unexpected.' Awareness is our protection. Amongst the greatest times of danger will be at the instant you are told good or bad news that comes as a surprise. This could be as simple as a job interview being cancelled because the interviewer is ill that day. You must not say 'I'll turn this day into a PRD'. No, no, ten thousand times no – the planning for those must follow the Oaken Rules or you will lapse into the old ways.

But we are not dodging any eventualities here and I said at the outset that there is a realpolitik that must be recognised that is associated with our programme that I don't want to avoid. We are human and The Trigger may be pulled particularly in the earliest days of our journey to getting better through PRDs. Remember what The Trigger is. It is an impulse that strikes without warning, cutting through your defences like a virus against which you aren't vaccinated. It is different to really wanting a drink which you can wait out or deploy tactical interventions to assuage the feeling. When I was drinking in the old way, at the end of a drinking phase when things had gotten to a point so bad I stopped the cycle, I told myself stop to dead and never drink again. During the days following I wanted a drink badly, but with a degree of rationally could reason out the consequences and take steps to make the pangs ease. These feelings decreased generally over time and in the evening I felt very pleased with myself that I accomplished what needed to be done that day. Then at a time where I was still enjoying and up to the challenge of being off booze The Trigger without warning would be pulled. There was always some justification it made as to why it had been pulled and the excuses it uses will be precisely tailored to every individual's personality traits and weaknesses. Here are some examples of the excuses it made to me via the booze imp on my shoulder, whispering in my ear. I had been off drinking for about two weeks and had a job interview in a week's time. The Trigger was pulled – 'you can have one last drinking day – provided you leave one exact full week to the interview', said the imp. It knew I am anal about my planning timescales being exact units of weeks and that I always told myself I needed a full calendar week off the booze for me to be at my freshest and most effective for an event where I absolutely needed to perform. Another example. I had stopped my drinking – had my last booze swallow forever at 11:59 59secs on New Year's Eve as told by my digi watch that I had set by an internet atomic clock an hour earlier. I went to bed full of the determination of stopping that this time of year engenders in many. Mid-morning on 1st Jan The Trigger was pulled. 'Come on it's a Bank Holiday for God's sake you can have a bit of fun today – no consequences,' advised my booze imp. That night determination to really stop this time kicked in with a vengeance. The next day it was pulled again. The imp's excuse? 'It's Bank Holiday in Scotland today – so erm, it OK for one last day' (I live in England but this sort of gave me some kind of permission and justification). Luckily, I didn't know at the time that 3rd Jan is a Bank Holiday in Japan! The reason for our strategy of PRDs is to remove the conditions through which The Trigger is pulled. We know we will drink again and this defers any cravings to a point in the future as our safety blanket. Be aware of the existence of The Trigger. Knowledge of it and analysis of the reasons why it has been pulled in the past, help to avoid the conditions which will lead to it being pulled on our first steps on the path. You have finally taken the key decision that the upsides to drinking are being outweighed by the downsides and have sought a path on which your drinking will reduce to zero. Once I had decided to embark on the path and started the planning of the first PRD – I have to tell you, The Trigger was never pulled again. There were times in SDs between PRDs that I wanted a drink – especially following unexpected pieces of good or bad news – but I was able to wait them out by deploying the tactical measures of my armoury. It wasn't pulled again and believe me I was the most hopeless drinker you could imagine – whose moral fibre was cut, time and time again. By recognising The Trigger, calling it out, isolating it and analysing it we know it, and by its recognition it can no longer hurt us.

But for some people The Trigger may be pulled once the process of PRD planning has started. It shouldn't happen but may and we have to be ready for all possibilities. No method is 100% infallible for everyone – that's why there are readmissions at booze clinics. If it were to happen in this programme it will likely be on very earliest steps of the path. If it does happen what do you do? First you never say to yourself – 'I'll make this a PRD'. No this is outside the process and be honest enough with yourself to realise this. You have to remind yourself as the day progresses that this is wrong and you are not following the processes to make you well – this at least until the la la, tiptoe through the tulips, nymphs and shepherds stage is reached and you are no longer concerned with such thoughts. You still have to buy enough piss so the red line of not drinking and driving is not crossed later in the day. Apart from this I could say please try to curb your intake, don't have a vast fat, crisp, chocolate laden munchy meal, don't sleep during the day and start boozing again when you wake up – but it won't make any difference. You will go through the usual stages of desperation later, probably even worse because you thought you were on the path and blew it. The morning after look at yourself in the mirror. Do you want to get back on the barricades again or have realised that for you are the upsides of drink are still higher that the downsides? You decide. If the former, either that day or the next, plan for the next PRD. Still record the naughty day in your diary and write down the units you consumed. You will need this for the preparation of the simple stats that chart your progress which I'll explain how to do in a little while.

Why does the Planned Relapse strategy work? There are other ways I might have reduced my alcohol intake once I'd decided the downsides of drinking were heavier in the balance other than using the PRD method controlled by the Oaken Rules. I may have limited the number of drinking days to a percentage of the month, say 20% of the days of a month to start with – and reduce this percentage over time. This would have set out a parameter to cap my drinking. But the problem with this method is the rules are loose enough to provide enough rope to hang oneself. This method does not allow our drinking to reduce to zero in a safe controlled way with the built-in mechanism to allow calm self-reflection that PRDs provide. I'd actually tried to use this method from time to time. Often I'd blow the all days allowed under the percentage cap consecutively right at the start of the month. This train of days of course would be indistinguishable to one of my old drinking cycles. But whichever part of the month I had a drink it definitely didn't stop at one day and I invariably used them all up in one go and then my mind was fully occupied and obsessed with the counting down to the first day of the next month. Mostly I failed to get to the next month and the old cycles kicked in again. The strategy of

PRDs integrated with the simple Oaken Rules is the best way to lose the stress of giving up allowing you the headroom to keep to the path.

The Three Oaken Rules of Planned Relapses:
First Oaken Rule: 'A PRD shall be no more than one day long'.
Second Oaken Rule: 'The time to the next PRD must be greater than it was to the last one'.
Third Oaken Rule: 'Plan only the next PRD'.

Oaken Rules for hearts of oak.

CHAPTER FOUR

TACTICAL WEAPONS

In the early days, the SDs between the PRDs can be hard even as the force of the addiction begins to wane. The overall campaign strategy is pushing us in the right direction but there are tactical weapons we can deploy when there are pangs that may occur when we see an advert for drink on TV or get sudden pieces of news that the dependency used to 'deal with'. How your day is structured led to periods within it where the danger of drinking was greater than others. If you work at home or are looking for a job at the moment (a job in itself and as worthwhile as paid work, don't let anyone tell you any different), these danger periods will be at different times and structured differently to someone who works in an office or factory where the type of job they have makes them full on for the day – but then they return home… Remember things get easier as we drink less, this really happens but help may be required on the way. These tactical weapons meant I did not stray from the strategy and believe me I was in the weakest bracket of giver uppers. It is important that you write down your tactical weapons – copy some direct from me, tailor others to suit you and add new ones if required. Always keep in mind the overall strategy. We use a diminishing number of Planned Relapse Days to make our drinking reduces toward zero. The Oaken Rules ensure this happens. We defer any cravings to these days. But we may require some tactical tools to help us along. These can be divided into Situation Tactical Weapons (STW) where we recognise or plan for a dangerous happenstance that would potentially lead us to drink, Thought Tactical Weapons (TTW) where we deploy counter thoughts to those that in the past would have led us to a drink, and Practical Tactical Weapons (PTW) that will physically stop us drinking by removing the problem at its source. Here are the Situation Tactical Weapons.

SITUATION TACTICAL WEAPONS
Unusual periods of stress
How to cope with fatalistic thoughts such as 'Covid is here, what the hell' – glug glug? Of course I get it – it's a sudden, unexpected duress of a kind that was totally unplanned for, where the security and freedoms of everyday life emanating from our supposedly impregnable modern technological society are called into question in a way we would never have believed could happen. What would I do now in these very rare situations? I wouldn't dwell on them as I have people who are dependent on me – the step up to the plate, roll up the sleeves, when the going gets tough the tough get going family of thoughts would come a calling – or rather I'd make them come to the fore in my mind. If I were to give in to

drink in these situations and leave the path – I think I would get myself into a hole that I may never dig myself out of. My lack of backbone would put me terminally beyond respect in my assessment of myself. Don't put yourself (or your loved ones) through it in such difficult times. Don't fall into the trap of thinking that in this time somehow the rules don't apply, or that the situation is so special that in this case alcohol is a useful coping mechanism. Alcohol substitutes real optimism grounded in rational thought with the false kind of la la country. It's important to see this. In these times you have to do your duty. Giving in to alcohol patently is dereliction. As the flight crew instructs in the pre-flight briefing – put on your own oxygen mask if needs be before helping others. You can only look after others by looking after yourself first. But then there will be real hope for the future grounded firmly in your pursuit of it as the very best you can be without all the physical and mental baggage of alcohol. When off booze problems become easier to face and solve. More than ever you must stick to the PRD strategy planning and observe the Oaken Rules. Draw confidence and strength from knowing you are sticking to the plan even in extra trying times.

Dealing with holidays
Be wary of being swept up by the thought that drinking brings good cheer as an excuse to make exceptions on public holidays so not to be left out. I'm not saying abolish Christmas, but this is the season when we might give in to good cheer for it 'only comes but once a year'. I remember Christmases which started out on their eves with roistering drink and cheer – but became more hellish as the twelve days progressed through too much food and booze leading to

enormous liver strain and copious stomach ejecta. By Twelfth Night the drummers drumming in my head signalled the start of a horrific post turkey cold turkey. The best Christmases I've had as an adult are those where I remained sober. For me it is easy to watch others drink and not be tempted so this was quite easy to follow, but for others it is a time of real danger. But if you have decided it's time to stop, don't blow it because your booze imp is wearing a Rudolph nose. Don't over think and brood upon Christmas or any other festival and get anxious as it arrives. Once you have embarked on the path it really is best you stick to it so plan accordingly. Alternatives for fulfilment should be found other than drink. There are a thousand other doors to let out life.

Of course, apart from Bank Holidays, the annual get away could be a source of great temptation even when the path is joined. I would say take great care in your planning of the two weeks, but I realise that you can't discount the beach option for example just because of the bar culture found there. Shore up for the shore. Be ready for the temptations – this in itself is not too difficult because you know exactly what to expect down to the very names of the watering holes at a favourite resort. Once again it really comes down to the question of do you really want to do something about your drinking? Are the downsides now greater for you? The chances are very high you will fall into the old cycles after you arrive home if you give into booze whilst on holiday. I know from experience. I remember the holidays I ruined through drink. Once, before I joined the path, on a short break to Malta I held out for two glorious fun and yes romantic days. Then on the second evening at a restaurant I had a bottle of beer with my wife's blessing. I immediately regretted it but it was too late. Later on I sneaked out of bed and scoured Valetta for a late opening convenience store. The rest of the holiday was devastated – I was even drinking miniature bottles of limoncello that I had secretly bought from the duty free shop in the 737's toilet flying home. What a loser, a bum. It was different when I was younger – the holidays with groups of people my age were founded on booze. The hangovers were just part of it to be slept off before the next bout. The week a bubble in which anything went. Later in life this very bubble is the greatest threat separated from normal life as it is. Chuck all the year's temptations into the fortnight is the form of the temptation. This would mean leaving the path. I wouldn't bet a rusted groat against anyone with a history of drink issues boozing again the hour after touchdown, and the old cycles reinitiated from then. I wouldn't think of an annual holiday in terms of booze temptation. Instead it's an opportunity to really discover yourself free from the pressures of normal everyday life. A little more forward planning of activities for you to look forward to once there is advisable. I know one thing. The best holidays I've had have been with my wife sober and on the path. Best by miles.

Specific occasions when you would be expected to drink
This STW is part strategic in that it dovetails with the process of Planned Relapse Days. There may be events planned where you would be expected to and expect to drink. You can still. You may say, 'hang on I thought we weren't supposed to drink other than in PRDs?' This will still hold true – what I am trying to do is address the realpolitik of life and drink. Initially, the fretting of not taking part in such events may be worse than drinking during them. When you have taken

more steps on the path you will have the will and confidence not to drink on any occasion, but early on you may wish to take such a day as a PRD. But once or twice only. PRDs really must be an introverted thing otherwise they won't work right. If you were to always take them on social occasions with friends, you'd be back to associating alcohol as the main route to real fun again and back to where you were before you knew it. Also you would repeatedly be presented with the quandary of which occasion do you choose to fit in with the Second Oaken Rule especially if you have a busy social calendar. You will almost inevitably break the Third Oaken Rule – plan one PRD at a time. PRDs give you a system to analyse what drinking really is – to lay bare in a controlled environment which lasts a day only that the downsides to drink are greater and to provide a contrast with the rest of your time where you are throwing off the addictive habits and becoming the best you can be. The other reason for them is to provide a safety blanket in which to ensure The Trigger isn't pulled. This gives you a system to never say never and tend to zero drinking. Best I give an example of when I had started on the path but a special event was coming up where I was expected to drink and did. I've alluded already to weekends away with some very good old university chums that happen about once per year. When we meet we let go by downloading a lot of what's been on our minds since we last met and in particular reminiscing about the days at college, in which beer always was a big part. If I hadn't drunk on these occasions the whole experience would be diminished hugely for them and it wouldn't have seemed right. I didn't want to be the cause of changing the spirit of these occasions so in this case I treated the first of them after I had embarked on the path as a PRD. I limited drinking to one day/evening only. I make sure it did not spill over into two (I stopped the alcohol before midnight) – that would be breaking the First Oaken Rule. The red lines were still in place – no drink driving, no drunken arguments or worse with third parties. Also in similar situations treat the RDs in the same way you usually would. Actually I felt just as terrible on the trip home on the morning after this event as I would on any day after I had taken drink. I was not quite sure why this was. I always enjoy seeing them and it was nothing to do with the weekend itself. Maybe the depressive effects of booze were heightened after the super intense fun and the tiredness of staying out so late. Whatever the reason, this day served as a PRD. If you have a circumstance to fill such as this then you may treat it as a PRD. But however you identify the occasions of the type I have just described, the Oaken Rules cannot be broken. PRDs taken in this way will not be as effective as those taken under controlled conditions. You will not be able to analyse your thoughts and feelings on the day in the same way. Therefore be very selective and sure of your ground in choosing them. This approach is a Tactical Weapon because it allows you to plan to keep within the Oaken Rules and fulfil your 'obligations' while you are still not as strong as you will become. As you progress on the path you'll find you have the will and confidence not to drink during such occasions.

Being around others drinking in general
The next STW involves planning for being around others who are drinking alcohol in general. These situations are inevitable – we can't and don't want to cut ourselves off from society after all. We are all different in how we're affected

under such circumstances. For me personally they weren't a problem. I can usually watch others boozing until the cows come home and don't feel a soupçon's scintilla of a pang. The exception would have been in the situation with weekends with my university friends – but I mitigated this very special circumstance as described above by turning it into a PRD. In all other instances I do not feel in anyway compromised by mineral water consumption when with others drinking. There are plenty of examples of this. A big one is work socialising – work nights out, boarded training courses, Christmas parties etc – in these I find it even very enjoyable not to drink when others are – not from a sense of superiority but because I can add more to the conversations in this way (and partly from a sense of superiority). With work colleagues I tell them I don't drink if pressed. If they don't like it for whatever reason then they don't like it – on this point I really couldn't care less what they think. Another instance is very rarely on birthdays or New Year's Eve or some such my wife will have a cocktail. She enjoys it, so what – it doesn't turn me into a slavering wreck. I'm not sure quite where my immunity of being infected from the drinking of others arises, but it certainly does exist. My boozing and desire to booze came from me and me alone – others drinking are a universe apart. So much for me – but there will be those of you who are more used to a drinking culture than I have experienced or you get regular, heavy peer pressure to drink – say for example sinking a few each week before a football match, or living in a village where the local is the centre of social life, or you work in one of those liquid lunch/drinking culture professions – I wouldn't presume to list all of them, certainly not judge! But the fact is you know the downsides to booze had the upper hand and you needed and wanted to take action and follow the strategy we have been discussing. If you don't the tipple tribulations will continue and increase. You know that. So you know you can't drink with the others. Revel in this! Find ways at these occasions to add more to them and the conversations within them than you ever did before. I suppose an example of the hardest situation would be repeat events where booze was felt necessary to enhance the experience – going to see the match every week a good example. I'll leave it to you about what you tell your friends – but why not say you're not drinking for health reasons (which is true) or weight loss. At any rate I wouldn't make a big song and dance about it – no great announcements, keep it understated – better for everyone. Be proud of yourself for the fortitude you show to the initial ribbing! This new reality with you will soon become the norm with them – and when all's said and done chances are you won't be the only one of the group not drinking. The fact is, if you want to get better there is no place for drinking in these situations – there's no value in trying to honey up that pill. However hard it is at first, it will get better and you have the PRDs on which to defer the cravings and pain. These are the only vehicles, nay the drays on which our burdens can be carried as they are progressively unloaded as time progresses.

THOUGHT TACTICAL WEAPONS

There are thoughts that you may have that in the past would have had you reaching for the can/bottle/flagon/flute. We need to recognise them so we can raise our shields by implementing the Thought Tactical Weapons when they happen. Here they are:

Receiving good or bad news
The first of the Thought Tactical Weapons is the readiness to deal with items of news that may turn your thoughts to wanting a drink. I have sited sudden pieces of news, good or bad, but include items of news you were expecting. If good these would in the past lead to a drink as a reward, or if bad to drown your sorrows. Examples of the latter could be the receipt of an e-mail saying you regretfully didn't get the job you thought you were nailed on for after interviewing so well, or the news of an illness striking a family member you care about. Similar is the anticipation of such an event, where you think you can't handle the waiting. The first defence against such occurrences is the knowledge of what you used to do in these situations before you decided to follow the path you are now on. Recognise the situation, remember how you used to deal with it, how monstrously worse your actions eventually made it and don't do it. Wait out the first few moments – these are the most dangerous. Then immediately undertake a period of reflection. If bad news, don't dwell on the news itself but plan immediately what you can do to rectify or mitigate the situation. If applicable (being told you didn't get the job), put your thinking into the plan B (always have a plan B) and physically pick yourself up. No one last drink to get over things – remember there is a PRD planned to help out. If someone else needs you like the illness of a person close to you, the immediate wanting a drink phase should be soon over as the need to help brings its own kind of fortitude. Believe me, when you go to bed that night you will thank providence for not having given in. After you have waited out the immediate danger and reconciled yourself that drinking is not going to happen today, the rest of the

day becomes much easier. People have not got jobs since time immemorial including big shots – its luck as much as anything and provided you had prepared as well as you could for the interview there can be no recriminations. If you didn't prepare as well as you could, do better next time. Of course there are other pieces of bad news other than not getting a job but it is a good example. Over time you will develop stronger and stronger immunity from wanting a drink immediately after news such as this. With sudden expected good news the reaction you had and will still have for a while is let's celebrate with a drink. In some ways this is more dangerous than bad news because you may feel so good about life due to the news that the usual guilty downsides of the boozing day may be swamped by it leading you to carry on. For me, after I had started on the path, the wanting of a drink after good news soon went away because I had readied myself for it and planned how I would react. Instead of feeling like getting sozzled instead I wanted to cash in on my good luck and press home the advantage to really secure that next rung up on the ladder of life – especially after a time of conceding rungs because of booze. Once again if you refrain from drinking after good news you will feel like something really special has been achieved come bed time and it will get much easier every time it occurs. The TTW is to be ready with your thought processes to be deployed in the event of sudden or even expected good or bad news. You may not quite anticipate the news itself but your plan for dealing with it can be set beforehand. I don't want to sound preachy here but I have been through it all and we want to be honest with ourselves that we have been dealing with these situations by using alcohol. We want to cover the realpolitik of when and why we want a drink and why the mixed metaphored best laid plans can go to pot if we aren't prepared.

The booze imp on your shoulder

Enter the booze imp again. There are lots of thoughts it slurs at you from your shoulder as it tries to tempt and entice you into drinking on the SDs in-between the PRDs especially early in the process. You will have your own examples – here are thoughts my imp has come up with together with the rebuttals and counter arguments.

'It's a fine morning, you're happy, so why should you not maximise your happiness by having a couple?' This is the first line that led me to drinking in the example I gave in Chapter One when The Trigger was pulled. Now my rebuttal is: 'a PRD is coming, I'll wait till then to explore booze and happiness.'

'Go on, not much on today – you can get away with it.' This is the second line my imp fed me in the Chapter One example. This is harder to counter unless we have the ready to go tactical weapon of filling up our day so booze isn't constantly thought about during it. This weapon is forged under the heading 'combating boredom' below. So the rebuttal is: 'yes, but I have a plan to have a useful day without drinking – any aches can be deferred anyway to my next PRD.'

'You need a pressure release today.' 'I'll get one on my next PRD.'

'C'mon just one – can't face the day alone.' 'I'm not alone – I got me babe!'

'You just need a time out for God's sake!' 'I'll get one on my next PRD.'

'Just get it all out of your system.' 'I can on my next PRD.'

'You have to get your kicks from somewhere!' What I've come to realise is the best kicks come from what's produced in an unaddled mind. What is a 'kick' anyway? A burst of pleasure narcotically induced – but pleasure with nothing behind it is bricks without straw. Shite without substance. It may be an alcohol enhanced celebration of good ideas I credit myself with. But what are the use of these if not carried through to realisation? Anyway, 'I can have a kick on my next PRD.'

'Why are you sucking all the fun from drinking?' 'I'm not, I'm passing on its terror.'

'Give yourself a short sharp shock.' 'This is what PRDs are for.'

'Give yourself back your freedom!' 'No, I'll keep removed from the cause of my slavery.'

'Actually the Belgian lager you drink has all the prerequisites of a health drink if you think about it. On the side of the tin it says it consists of pure water, malted barley, maize and hops. I'm very sorry but you can't get much healthier than that – a superfood if ever there was one.' This one's not worth dignifying with an answer. Suffice it to say that argument's about as thin as discount supermarket's own brand bog roll.

'You want the day to go quick.' But there will be another sunrise tomorrow and the day after. If I want my time to go quick, then why not save a step and take it out of the equation altogether by slashing my wrists? How can I not handle the short enough time I have on the planet? 'No, better being alive where I can do some good. I'll lean on my next PRD.'

'You want to get back to your roots – for one day be the real you.' OK completely illogical but I'll try – I put that one in because my imp said it a few times. The real me is the one before I knew booze. Boozing has led me to near ruin. If you think how you feel when boozing is the real you, there's a problem. But you know you were never at your best when boozing as the sorry catalogue of lost opportunities and failed projects attests. So my response: 'I have the next PRD to take a dose of the 'real me' and compare him to the person I am becoming sans sauce.'

'Free your head – have a really creative day.' 'Well I can try on my next PRD – but aren't getting my hopes up as to the quality of my output!' I have come to find that this thought is especially bogus. Most of the best work you do is when your brain is free from booze and operating at its best level. If you need to be convinced of this devote some time during the first few PRDs to 'being creative'. This is what I did – but it soon stopped as I found the vast majority of the 'work' I did to be gobbledegook if I could read it at all. This stopped the danger of planning PRDs to be my creative days and scheduling them at regular intervals to be such. This is not what they are for – they should be the future deferrals of wanting a drink, something to put the weight of cravings on to – that the Oaken Rules guarantee become less over time. In themselves they should and must be worthless days – spent drinking for its own sake but after to be analysed and learnt from. Wanting a drink to be creative is a bad excuse we make to ourselves in justification. Recognise this and realise as I did that the best work is done when you are free of intoxicating, addling agents.

'**Churchill** (there are others you can substitute with other justifications) **took a lot of alcohol each day even during the war – look what he achieved with it.**' This excuse is pernicious and ultimately inappropriate. First there is at least anecdotal evidence to suggest that he did not drink as much as the myth suggests – but there is little doubt that he took rather a lot daily. That the exception proves the rule is a little lazy for our need to understand here. I can't explain why Churchill performed so effectively even with alcohol. I obviously never knew him and haven't read any of the esteemed biographies – so all I've got is anecdotal snippets which cannot give the full picture. I can speculate that he was completely driven towards a certain all encompassing goal. He had an extensive team of doers that could carry out the details of his strategies. It's true that he did suffer with his 'black dog' of depression that drink would probably have fuelled. It's best to say there have been some important instances in history where it just happened and on the face of it there were no major detrimental consequences of alcohol to the important and singular task at hand. My imp used to often feed me this line. I realised that Churchill was exceptional and focussed on a goal so well defined and important that the dependency was a fact that had to be carried with him in those times without his allowing it to be too detrimental. His constitution certainly contained more iron than mine. Well maybe after all it is best to say the exception proves the rule. We can't know others with regard to their boozing but we do know ourselves. We know how it affects our performance which is why we have decided to do something about it.

I sometimes used to end a period of abstinence when a drinking song was played at a party say. The imp said **'oh go**

on get into the swing of it for Christ's sake.' I remember at a more scholarly do partaking in a group roistering recital of the poem by Henry Aldrich – *Reasons for Drinking*:

'If all be true that I do think,

There are five reasons we should drink:

Good wine – a friend – or being dry;

Or lest we should be by and by;

Or any other reason why'.

My imp said 'he's right you know' and I was off before I knew it. When you know an event is coming where drink will flow and is recognised as being integral to the event – a wedding, wake, sport club dinner – be prepared. Fortify yourself with the planning you have made in the PRD process which is all your work and highly personal to yourself.

These were some of the deviant lines my booze imp fed me and how I countered them. Write down and remember your own counters so to be prepared when the lines come as they will. This is the TTW to deploy against the imp. Think about the arguments yours will try it on with, so when it does you can tell it to sod off.

Combating boredom

Another Thought Tactical Weapon to discuss – one equipped with multiple warheads is how to combat boredom. Boredom is a vexed subject in that we often cite it as a reason why we start drinking if the day stretches out before us and it appears it can't be filled any other way (certainly I did). I prefer to frame it now though as an excuse we give ourselves to drink. A day drinking is a day lost and worse it promises the despair of the aftermath – what is the point of a string of useless days going ever quicker, speeding you to your end? It is true, though, that in the earliest days of our path time can weigh heavily upon us. On the first steps the tactical weapon to deploy is preparedness for when the feeling of boredom arises. Be prepared to summon your fortitude and stoicism when a day starts and you are not sure how to fill it. In the early days of your path to throwing alcohol just keeping to the path is the most important thing. You may be someone who likes to achieve something every day – to move their life on and do all they can to prepare for the next rung on life's ladder. But at this early stage it's OK, you don't have to achieve every day. These are the earliest stages where we set the foundations for a better life. For now, if you have days where you're not doing anything in particular, it's fine. You are not drinking, that's the main thing. Bugger all is good.

What we can do though, in these early days, is plan to arrange our time so boredom is not a problem. For me boredom manifested itself as brooding in the periods of time in which I had very little to do. I had accepted that the downsides of drink had now outweighed the upsides and I had started on the path described herein. This means that I wasn't gasping all the time and had built up enough fortitude reserves for me to keep to the plan. But these brooding periods were a problem to my well-being and caused blockages to the optimal flow of performance in mind and body. So when a day was coming that would be quite empty and therefore dangerous I thought about all the tasks that I would like to see addressed during it so it could be more full. At about five o' clock the day before I would write them down – only subject headings nothing too detailed. Then the next day, the potential boredom day, even if I was slightly paralysed by the brooding, there was a checklist of tasks that I could cross off during it to ensure the day was filled. In those early days I did not set myself a rigid timetable. Obviously if out at work or working from home your timetable of tasks and meetings often takes care of filling the day – but not always and the days I'm dealing with here are those when there's not much in the work diary or you are out of work or just have time on your hands. It helped me to do the task I felt like doing at the time, not necessarily in the order I was wont to do it. There was an element of keeping myself busy for busy's sake I admit – but I didn't drink nor did I think much about it. So for example when I woke up after all ablutions (you have to do those at the usual time each day), I would usually go and check my e-mails on my computer. I then did what I felt like when I felt like doing it. So I might have done some yard work first if that took my fancy. Then I might go for a run, then I might be ready for an intensive work session on the laptop. Or I might first go to the supermarket for the meal stuff my wife had written me down to get. Perhaps then I'd watch half a film I'd recorded or read a couple of chapters of my novel. Books whether fact or fiction are very good for these days – they speak directly to you from down the ages and take your mind off somewhere else completely. Then I may perambulate Peggy. Then I would take the rubbish out and make a marmite, squeezy cheese, peanut butter and dripping sandwich (on rye). At the conclusion of each task I immediately selected the next one, thinking about it only and not looking further than my nose. Take care of the minutes and the hours take care of themselves. I was letting the day unfold as it should – going with the flow of my internal rhythms doing things that felt right at the time. I used to be so rigid in my thoughts – a time for everything and everything at its proper time. I would get myself into a tiz if the routine was broken and would stress about completing the most mundane tasks at their allotted time. When I embarked on the path I knew these traits were if not drink originated then drink exacerbated and I changed. After embarkation, the only thing I knew at the commencement of a day with the potential for boredom was that I had now enough tasks to fill it because I had written them down the evening before – so nothing to worry about. By thinking about only the next job the day became a creeping barrage, in WW1 parlance, of tasks – each one moving me a bit further forward in time. No time for brooding in a Creeping Barrage – you have to keep moving until the day's objectives are taken. Try this approach. Boredom is bogus there is always something to do. Useful thought and self reflection are also shells that should be part of your barrage – add them to your inventory if you don't have enough physical stuff to do. But in the early days of the path don't let boredom lead to temptation, there is no reason for this and it isn't an excuse – ring fence it and recognise it for what it is. Deploy the tactical weapon that is the Creeping Barrage method. Use the comfort blanket of the next PRD and be aware that things get easier as the path is followed. Have faith in your ability to succeed.

Not getting caught out

Be Prepared. In *Scouting For Boys* Baden-Powell wrote that to Be Prepared means 'you are always in a state of readiness in mind and body to do your duty'. Early on the path, every day in the evening have a quick but serious think about what the danger points in the probable next day's events are and prepare for them. My signature example is that of the haylage. Another example: in the old days before the path, after a period of abstinence, I would be allowed out to the shops on my own for various needed items with my debit card. Often the Trigger wouldn't believe its good luck – it would seize its opportunity and booze would be procured. In the early days of the path I thought through the probability of my being alone out with my card the next day. This prep saved me from disaster more than once as I was girded but at peace when the time came to leave the house encarded.

Planning for a goal

Medium term planning for a specific event really helps you to forget all drink related thoughts and feelings as you aim for the goal especially in the early days of the path. By medium term I mean an event that is up to one month over the horizon. It is an event where you will have to be at the top of your game and will have to put some work in prior to it. Examples are a job interview, being head planner for a friend's wedding, an after dinner speech, a work presentation to a critically important new client, your first stand up routine to an audience. There are usually such things on all our radars at quite regular intervals. Even if there aren't any really do or die big ones there is usually something we don't want to mess up and plan properly for. These could be organising a day out at the coast for a group of seniors or a birthday party for your child. They may also be physical such as a charity fun run. Set the status of such events to an 'official medium term goal'. Give it this status because it then becomes a Tactical Weapon in your arsenal against drink. Let the time you set aside for it per day be part of your Creeping Barrage of tasks if needs be. Nothing focuses greater than fear of failure – but once you have acknowledged this don't frame the event in such terms. Let all your thoughts be positive and focussed on doing your very best on the day. We can't get the job every time – we can't know the calibre, focus and competency of the interviewer/s on the day for starters. But once the medium-term goal is made official in our thoughts and plans we can work towards it with full gusto and vigour, destroying drink's influence. Even in events where there is a danger of total failure, such as the job interview, you will know you have done your very best and have done the groundwork to be more effective at your next one. Some goals are more of an artificial construct. One month out from my birthday I always redouble my weight loss programme, fitness regime etc to feel my best for the day that marks another log being chucked on the fire from the ever-dwindling pile. Medium terms planning is a great addition to your armoury to take the mind off you know what, so give each event its label and plan to be the best you can on the day.

Doing it for others
The focus of this guide is to beat alcohol using all your individual resources physical and mental. I knew in order for any solution to work I needed to plan and execute it myself. Individual total war without distraction. This is why I knew solutions that utilise group sessions as a key pillar would not work with me. Supporting strangers was not an option. The problems were within me and I could only really articulate them to myself and be truthful to myself. With others I would have toned down some truths or lied or invented things or just tried to make myself look as good or at least, least bad as possible. It might have been temporarily good to

get things off my chest but wouldn't have stuck and knowing me I would have probably wanted a drink even more the instant I got home because of my just-been-confessed state of grace. Absolved, slate clean, glug glug. The getting off drink – the planning of PRDs, the selection and application of the tactical weapons, the logging of progress is something that you should own and manage as a person who reconciles the problem and solution within. In this way it will stick and all the life boosting feelings of accomplishment are yours alone. The details of the journey on the path, especially the first steps, should not be the subject of announcements to the outside world in general. There are exceptions that you may manage and inform as you wish. These are very close family and friends. My wife is my primary example. She bore the brunt of the bad bits of my drinking (to her there were no good of course) and it was only right that when I embarked on the path I was able to give her hope of better times. I did not sit her down and explain the process I had decided upon in detail. This would have compromised the need for it to be highly personal and that the ins and outs should be known only to me – it would only fully work if this covenant to myself was kept. I did however give signals that I was getting a lot better – telling her how much better I was feeling. We no longer had the really damaging rows the causes of which were laid exclusively at the foot of drink (and me). I also made sure as far as I could, that we didn't row full stop. It was actually great to see how when I didn't drink we didn't row. Consciously not being argumentative, looking for trouble or in any other way being disagreeable is necessary for your well-being and can be thought of and packaged up as an official Tactical Weapon. Working on your key relationships when you have decided to do something about your drinking by following the process herein helps to ensure its success. She could see that I was not drinking and this made her happier. Making her happy is a primary goal of my life. Her happiness once attained or improved must be maintained. Really trying to cut out the grouchiness with loved ones helps us to carry on, on the path. As well as cutting out the bad, plan the good signals you want to give out and how and when you want to deploy them. These might be regular exclamations such as 'wow I feel really great today' or the delivery of more surprises and spontaneity like 'want to go for a bit of a drive' or the buying of flowers (that demonstrably are no longer a means of apology). These are some of mine – you can develop your own. The arrangement of PRDs was an area where if I did not lie, I did hold back some truths, but the ultimate benefits outweighed the deceit. So, as I have mentioned, I often chose a hotel room for a PRD on the premise I was working away. I chose others to be taken at home when she was away visiting family or friends. It is essential the fact that a particular day is a PRD is kept cloaked from all but you or it loses all its value.

So although the central tenet of this guide is getting yourself better as an individual, doing it for others helps us keep to the path – a tactical weapon that we can think about when required to shore us up especially in the early days. Then it will be especially effective because any damage done due to the addiction is still fresh. Doing it for others is therefore an effective addition to your armoury. Letting your loved ones know you are improving through signals and deeds you consciously plan for and deliver, gives both parties encouragement. I would plan 'spontaneous' acts for my wife the day before by including them in the tasks I had to perform the next day. She was so pleased that I was obviously not drinking. The possibilities were opening up and becoming apparent to us each in our own heads. I was succeeding in my complimentary goal of 'doing it for her' by my main goal of 'doing it for me'. My wife, to my great fortune, was genuinely into us being together – what people call love I suppose – no faking it, and could see that our union would now be far more of a success. But the realisation that the downsides of booze were outweighing the benefits was mine alone to experience as was the planning and deployment of the route to becoming the best I could be. Yet the experience of another's joy from the improvements in how you present yourself to the world and to them in particular, rightly motivates you to stride ever more confidently forward.

PRACTICAL TACTICAL WEAPONS

Now we design and build of third part of our tactical arsenal – the Practical Tactical Weapons. These can be thought of as tools that can be quickly deployed to ensure we can't physically drink. Some may even be deployed as emergency measures. As with the other tactical weapons dealt with above we require them less as the path progresses. But early on sometimes we may experience weakness and these measures will ensure no drops of ethanol violate our oesophagi.

Measures to physically stop yourself from drinking
- Don't keep any booze in the house. Obvious but must be said. Anyone really close to you living in the same house will understand the temptation must be removed. If you expect guests where it would be awkward not to offer

them something, buy it before they arrive and dump the excess after they leave. If you have a flat share it's harder but try your best to influence others to secrete theirs where you would not go – in their room for example or their car. If it's really a drinking flat share it may be time to find another.

- When shopping at the supermarket route yourself not through the drink aisles – take the extra steps and turn in at condiments. I used to look at my hands and instruct them not to pick up cans and take them to the checkout. Do not have to say this hand hath offended.
- Early on in my journey there were some days that I have already classed as potential boredom days. I successfully used the Creeping Barrage technique of filling up my day as already described. However, when such a day was coming up I needed to make absolutely sure. This is when I gave my wallet to my wife the night before and asked her to keep it until the mid of day next. This needs to be done in the right way. First it must be done the evening before. This is so you will have reconciled yourself by the next morning that you have no means to drink and will be relaxed about it, no pangs – they've been planned away. When you give the wallet or purse to your nominated person make sure all your means of purchase will be unavailable to you. I think you can broadly guess what I'm going to say next. Once, before I started on my path, I gave my wallet to my wife the night before. The next morning found me looking down the back of the sofa for coins and I added them to the parking change I had left in the car. There was enough for eight cans from a discount supermarket. The supermarket staff

looked on appalled as it took me ten minutes to get the coins into the self service machine, retrying repeatedly with the rejected coins and swearing. So make sure ALL possibilities are covered. Also I have to say to my eternal shame I once tried to load a fake $1M dollar bill (with John Wayne on it) my wife had bought me for my birthday into the machine. I'd like to say it took it for the beer and gave me every penny it had in it for change plus an IOU for $999,880 – but it didn't. The next point re wallet/purse giving up is even more important. When taking this action you must make a solemn covenant with yourself that you will not ask/beg/scream for your card back before the allotted time. This is a red line. If you tear the house apart looking for it or threaten the person you entrusted with helping you by doing this you really do risk losing everything. If you do this then you are not ready in your own mind to give up drink yet. But the tactic is effective in the early days of your journey on the path. Do not become dependent on this device however as it gives stress to the other. Use it only when you perceive the danger will be real on a particular day. As you progress on the path you will soon reach a point where this measure is no longer needed.

- Try not to substitute one form of stimulant for another. We want to get off the whole thing of having to be stimulated by foreign agents designed for the task. So don't spend the start of each day fitting most of your surface area with nicotine patches. In themselves they're not going to harm you massively but we are trying to make a philosophical change within ourselves here – as well as a change that will result in a longer life and mental well-being. This philosophical change will be the root of our increased happiness – real happiness – not the faux alcohol induced variety. We want to be proud that we can manufacture this proper happiness within ourselves without recourse to any kind of stimulant that is just a substitute for booze. If we become as dependant on things like nicotine patches, it is only a small step to reverting to the other kind of artificial stimulant we know – booze. No, think about the pure happiness we generate using our internal resources unencumbered as a root. 'Give me but one firm spot to stand, and I will move the earth,' said Archimedes. In summary – don't use nicotine patches or their ilk, or your ability to move the earth will be severely curtailed.

- Tea and coffee are OK but don't overdo the caffeine drinks either especially in the early days. Don't be over stimulated so take them in moderation. Be smart enough to know what moderation means to you. Basically don't pour rivers of coffee down your gullet in an attempt to 'get to the level' of boozing stimulus. If you find yourself doing this stop and remind yourself of your next PRD. I have never drunk the fizzy caffeine laden drinks available but know enough anecdotally to advise to keep off them early on the path.
- Take up smoking or vaping? – no way, no how, end of.
- Fizzy drinks of the diet kind can be very useful in this period – especially if your alcoholic drink of choice was fizzy (or you added soda water to it). In the early days I would knock back tins of diet cola of various types in the morning. It felt like the old stuff in my gob. I actually enjoyed noting that the feeling of it going down was the

same but that of progressive inebriation was not. As I could feel I wasn't becoming wrecked, I knew I would be spared the anguish later. By this substitution I felt I had got one over on booze. The mere act of opening a tin and pouring down something fizzy stopped pangs in their tracks or at least gave me something to do whilst waiting out the danger moments. So select your favourite non sugarful/caffeine laden tipple that feels close to the sensation of your alcoholic tipple as a PTW. By the way I don't include non or low alcohol beer or wine in this. I know the manufacturers mean well but I find them vile. Also they would be the worst of all possible worlds. You would be self torturing with stuff that reminded you at each swallow of the stuff you were giving up. Unless you positively enjoy self flagellation, I honestly wouldn't bother.

- Using food tactically is effective. Even in the old days if I ate a big meal, I never felt like drinking afterwards – digestifs were as do-do to me. So a tactic I used when I believed I was in danger was to eat a big meal. In the morning this meant visiting the golden arches place or similar and stuffing. This can't be just pushing food in to push pangs out but should be enjoyable too. So choose substantial foods that are designed to make you maximise your intake while still making it enjoyable. Fast food is ideal for this. Remember this is a practical tactical step that may not be great in itself but is a million times better than the alternative. I'm not going into the ins and outs of the nutritional value of fast food because it's irrelevant for the purpose we have assigned it here. The food needs to be weighty enough to do the job it's supposed to do – cutting out alcohol cravings. Crisps, nuts, chocolate won't work – not weighty enough – you simply can't get the volume in with these fast enough. Plus these are the drink complimentary foods you won't want to be reminded of. The concept of using food tactically like this isn't particularly pleasant and you certainly long term won't be operating a glugging for gluttony exchange programme – but if it works just once in the early days this paragraph has been worth the reading.

- The previous PTW uses food as a quick fix to dampen a particular dangerous instance. Thinking longer term we must concentrate on good diet. Bad diet and alcoholism go hand in hand. Think chocolate, crisps, peanut butter, squeezy cheese and lard spread on doughnuts time and again. This isn't a guide that helps with what to eat to ensure a good diet – there are plenty of books out there that do that. I can only tell you how my diet changed when I embarked on the path. The embarkation became not just a route to throwing drink but a stimulus for planning my well-being, performance optimisation and life expectancy maximisation by any and all means. Alcohol carries a lot of calories – certain drinks such as Advocaat exacerbate this with their delish creaminess. I used to neck two bottles of this drink on 'special occasions'. I remember once being the victim of a buy 2 get 1 free offer for a German discount supermarket parody of the ancient Dutch product. I turned a nostalgic childhood Christmassy treat into a vomit fest as my world turned into a hideous universe of yellow out of my mouth, eyes and nose. I digress, my point is I ingested more calories that day than the grains of sand at Southport. My weight yo-yoed like mad when I was drinking but on average I was about two and a half stones overweight. Whichever way you look at it – 35 pounds, 16 kilos – it's a shed load. So when I had decided the downsides of drinking were outweighing the good, the desire for weight loss gave me complimentary momentum in the overall fight. You may not need to lose weight but eating healthier is something we can pretty much all do from our baseline. You can still eat things you like out of the really bad categories – during the very first days of the path don't make yourself miserable through weight loss and food choices – but make some tweaks and plan your meals and diet progressively nudging along the improvements. This is a good daily bit of work to do and is great on a potentially dangerous boredom day when it can be part of your Creeping Barrage. I ate rice crackers aplenty but also added worthwhile cals back in – two squares of 99% dark chocolate per day. This is the best food for detoxing our bodies by loads. I believe over time I have felt a real difference with this. Then there's supplements. Some people poo poo supplements. It's true if you take too many your body just flushes em out unused – in the poo poo. But I think if you use them wisely and sparingly they really help in your bodily improvement. For example I want to maximise the efficiency and power of my brain, partly because the bar is set low for it, partly because I had been destroying its cells on a regular basis. So now I employ three high strength omega 3 capsules per day. I also take a combined magnesium, glucosamine and calcium pill for my musculoskeletal system. I'd read magnesium helps with cramp – so I started taking it even before I had decided to do something about my drinking. After a couple of days into the drinking cycle I used to get the most fearful cramp. It was though I'd copped a glimpse of Medusa and was progressively turning to stone – so hard and tight did my calves especially become. Some pains are exquisite this was just plain excruciating. Calves, ankles, fingers, stomach muscles, neck, erm privates, at various points throughout the day and night – nasty. So plan a better diet and see where supplements can help to improve your body and good feelings about yourself. All the steps we take to this end will feed off each other on our journey of improvement.

- Exercise and striving to be as healthy as you can be is one of if not the most important of the Practical Tactical Weapons in your armoury. It becomes a project for you that runs parallel and complimentary to your journey off drink. For me my mood had a grapple iron linked to my health. The absolute worst times used to be when during a drinking cycle I neglected exercise leading to an ever-deepening orbit around the black hole that my thrusters sometimes only just freed me from. Bits of me in the feet/leg region would swell up from gouty type conditions which meant I was hobbling around for a large proportion of my time – when one joint was recovered, the over compensation I had given it when walking meant another joint would swell up in turn, until they all had a go in an all too familiar sequence. It would be a couple of weeks off booze before I had recovered enough to walk properly. Then my overall fitness had dropped so when I began to use the gym again I felt I was back to square one. I would be going great guns for a time then have a prolonged drinking session with associated swelling and would be right back where I started. My self esteem took repeated bum whackings. When I had chosen to follow the path the accompanying upward curve on my exercise regime and fitness complimented and fed off my drink reduction planning so well. Working out an exercise regime is key to maximising your mind/body effectiveness while coming off booze. We all have differing abilities in terms of what we can do to exercise. But we can all do something and plan to improve what we do over time. It is very important that we improve our health through exercise, hand in hand with following the path. So please work on your exercise plan.

- Learning a new skill is a great Practical Tactical Weapon to deploy such as night school classes or buying a language course. If you do this, make sure it's something you'll see through and don't bite off more than you can chew. If it becomes a bind or you jack it in it could become dangerous. We don't want to put ourselves in a position of feeling failure which could have been avoided. Alcohol used to 'deal with' failure and we don't want to link the two and feel tempted to drink again because of it.
- Use self-peer pressure, the best there is. Find and keep close your favourite photo of yourself before you knew drink – preferably you're looking directly out of the picture and alone. Hopefully you'll not be too young for you to remember how you were then! Try to be true to that impless person when tempted.

A discourse on the damaging effects of alcohol to the human body

In the year before I decided to embark on the path I was experiencing new symptoms that indicated things could be getting quite worse health wise. For example instances of swelling of feet or rather a tinge of swelling which I would foolishly exercise on that would lead to a full blown swelling event that would keep me hobbling for days, the inflammation switching from muscle to muscle in sympathy. Consequently I couldn't do my usual cardio activity of cross training. I couldn't even spend decent time on my backside on the rowing machine because of the soreness. I was also getting regular bouts of extreme soreness in the tips of the bones in my knuckles, elbows and shoulder blades. The dip in my ability to exercise would be shadowed by a drop in my mental well-being as with me one to a large extent depends on the other. All these symptoms would go away after a period not drinking and I was able to manage them by strengthening the susceptible muscles in nondrinking periods. Yet I found that when I started to drink again, anymore than two consecutive days would lead to a re-swelling somewhere on my person. Of course as long as I had ever been drinking I had experienced the usual effects the morning after – dry mouth, thumping heartbeat (the Tubal Cains), confusion, cramp etc. When these happen every day over a prolonged drinking session you don't need anyone to tell you your system is being put under enormous pressure. Now we'll have a look at these conditions in more detail to see what damage they are symptomatic of. Being aware of and concerned about these is a good Practical Tactical Weapon to deploy on the path. These conditions are made worse when the drinking patterns are chronic. Because of the Oaken Rules governing PRD planning – this chronic aspect is removed. Just before I embarked on the path as I mentioned I was experiencing new conditions. Let's not pussyfoot around – the brontosauruses in my lounge were liver cirrhosis and heart disease. I reckon I dodged them starting to get advanced without much time left. We'll have a look then at cirrhosis and heart disease – we have to. Finally we will check out how alcohol affects the immune system – vital to counter with new viruses knocking about.

Dry Mouth
Dry Mouth has actually a proper name – Xerostomia. If it gets a name its bad. It covers needing to drink water heavily upon waking, not making enough saliva to talk with clarity in the morning and even foul breath after frequent high intake of booze. You can also have dry mouth for a time after you have stopped drinking – I used to get this for one or two days after the old drinking cycles. Dry mouth is caused by dehydration – the course of fluids in your body changes after drinking alcohol. Our kidneys don't send the water back to the body because of the diuretic nature of booze, and instead the water is expelled which triggers our thirst and extra loo visits. When we're drinking alcohol we are not taking up enough water – this is obviously truer the more concentrated the alcohol we take, sprits neat being the worst for this. So we don't have enough water in the bloodstream and the body takes it where it can, diverting it from saliva production. It also takes it from the cells. The body must do this to maintain blood pressure which supplies organs with oxygen – it knows it has to prioritise this to prevent organ

failure. The cells which copped it because of this process are sucked dry. These cells include those from the liver, kidneys and brain. These organs will be damaged if too much water is dragged from their cells. The liver is especially at risk. It processes liquids and food, removing toxins that could harm the body. Continued chronic alcohol use can take a toll on the liver, eventually making it unable to function properly. When the liver can't do its job, alcohol can dehydrate the body even more than it usually does. On a PRD, before going to bed, drink lots of water and have some handy if you wake during the night.

Pounding Heart
Several hours after finishing drinking, the alcohol raises the body's level of epinephrine, a stress hormone that increases the heart rate and generally stimulates the body, which results in waking up during the night and the Tubal Cains. Even before turning in, when you are drinking, alcohol makes blood vessels in the skin dilate, which means the heart has to pump more blood to keep the same amount circulating through the rest of the body. It does this by beating a little harder and faster in order to keep up. Now if you eat a big meal also before going to bed the heart has to work even harder to provide the blood to the digestive processes. Given all this is there any wonder my chest would ache with the sheer effort the poor bloody thing had to put in. I could feel mine at the limit of its tolerance and it scared me to bits.

Body Chemistry
I'll never forget the morning after my final old drinking cycle before starting on the path. I was lying in bed in the usual

state of torture hardly being able to comprehend the sheer quantity of adrenalin my system was pumping. At every instance of early morning sound – birdsong, branches rustling and the creaks of the house as it warmed and expanded, I recoiled in fear and ejected another spurt of adrenalin. At least my adrenal glands are working if everything else is wonky I thought. I also thought I'm going to pay heavily for this so set out to find out a bit more about boozing and adrenalin production and the whole question of how our body chemistry is affected. Well when you start drinking, it turns out that the alcohol affects the gamma-aminobutyric acid (GABA) receptor, which is the main inhibitor of the central nervous system. At the commencement of the drinking session this is what causes the feeling of well-being and joy. As you drink more the brain stimulant glutamate which causes anxiety is suppressed. So the more blitzed you get the less anxiety and inhibitions you feel. Glutamate is also important for fixing memories in your brain which is why you can't remember some of your antics the morning after. Even though you are doing your best to mess it up, the body always tries to restore balance so takes a deep breath and does what it can to reach equilibrium with respect to getting the GABA levels down and increasing glutamate. So when the drinking session has stopped (and most likely when you're in bed), the body produces a big hit of glutamate whilst holding back the GABA. This is what causes the fear, anxiety and anguish. Another mess up in body chemistry caused by the booze is it causes the body to produce more adrenaline that in turn causes the stress feeling when it hits the brain. If you are prone to feelings of guilt because of your drinking, this effect of moving from one extreme to the other in your mood as a result of compensations of chemical production induced by the body because of the alcohol consumption brings it on badly. Not everyone is affected the same way – it depends on your character to start with. I'm very prone to feelings of guilt – maybe this is why at my worst I felt almost suicidal in my despair. The way I see it though, better this than to be so cocksure of yourself and your body's resilience to booze that you carry on as always then wonder why you've wound up in the back of an ambulance with liver failure. Make guilt work for you! Age or rather experience is also a factor of how we are affected by these chemical imbalances. When I was a kid I never felt this stress the morning after. I couldn't give a toss about the downsides of drink – I'd had no real experience of them except the usual pissing in the fountains of youth. Another chemical imbalance, if all that wasn't enough, is drinking heavily increases the production of the hormone cortisol via the adrenal glands and affects how we respond to stress – the fight or flight thing. When stewing in bed after a session we can do neither, so the stewing is exacerbated. But it's worse – overproduction of cortisol over a period of time can have other consequences such as increased blood pressure and detrimental effects on other of your body's doings such as the central nervous system, reproductive and digestive systems. Sudden alcohol withdrawal also raises cortisol levels and with it stress. This can lead to the feelings of bleak hopelessness of a drinking dead stop – and makes the PRDs even more of a necessary buttress. GABA, glutamate, adrenalin and cortisol yo-yoing like mad – with all this going on is it any wonder you feel less than tip top with drink? But what a great tactical weapon to have in your armoury on your journey on the path – the knowledge of what the imbalances of these chemicals are doing to your brain, any brain not just yours. To see booze for what it is – the senseless causation of suffering because a foreign narcotic agent is fannying about with your precious workings, is so powerful in countering its pull. Be aware of why you are brooding in the small hours. It's the imbalance of your chemicals that's the cause. Remove drink, your body returns to equilibrium and the brooding stops. Remind yourself of this mid-brood and you'll be all ready to be released for good by embarking on the path.

Musculoskeletal Effects
I've mentioned bits of me swelling up due to drink. Alcohol triggers gout and causes it to recur again and again. Unfortunately my choice of booze didn't help. Some alcoholic drinks contain large amounts of purines, compounds which break down to uric acid. Beer is one of these drinks. Uric acid crystals around the joints are the cause of gout. This condition is more prevalent in men – but of course women should not be complacent – if booze doesn't get you one way it'll get you another. Swelling in the joints started to affect me in the last year or so of my old heavy drinking cycles. It never appeared while I was actually drinking, usually the day after when due to the physical and mental effects of withdrawal my bones and joints would feel over sensitive and achy in gerneral and I would feel stiff as a varnished eel. I would feel a tinge at the extremity of some bone or in a joint with the purest dread in my breast because I knew I was in for a rough spell. Any hard exercise on the day after stopping especially involving my legs would guarantee an attack. Then as already described I would have the misery of hobbling about for weeks sometimes, knowing I was becoming ever more

unfit. So there's no question this gouty effect and swelling was caused by my drinking. When not drinking I could eat whatever rich food I liked and no attack was triggered. I had learnt from the doctor that excessive, chronic drinking can also cause death of bone tissue or avascular necrosis. Anything with the prefix *necro* in its title is very bad. It's no less than the death of bone tissue caused by a lack of blood supply to affected areas. Tiny cracks can appear in the bones of your hip, knee, shoulder, hands and feet. The extreme soreness I had from time to time in the very tips of my shoulder blade, kneecaps and elbows may have been caused by this – once again it only came on the day after drinking periods. Alcohol may also inrease the risk of osteoarthritis, a degenerative joint disease. If I hadn't started on the path I would have definitely have been up for this I reckon because arthritis runs in my family anyway.

Chronic heavy boozing can also affect the muscles via a condition called myopathy. This causes pain and tenderness in the muscles and even progressive weakness. The most common symptoms are cramping and muscle twitches and spasms, old friends to me who thankfully don't visit as much anymore. But you can get atrophy – loss of muscle mass as well. I have always tried when possible to keep my muscles strong through cardiovascular exercises and weight training. That I started this quite young was because even then in the back of my mind I knew I had to do something to counter my alcohol abuse or else I would be in trouble in not much later life. I think this has saved me to a large extent from atrophy. I really believe exercise is doubly important and necessary to the drinker, its import continuing when the path is joined. Without it I would be a fathom under now, of this I'm convinced. This is because a further symptom of alcoholic myopathy is cardiomyopathy or weakening of the heart muscle. The muscle is thinned leading in turn to the risk of heart attack and stroke. My heart was exposed to the double whammy of cardiomyopathy and the Tubal Cains. One of the most precious bits of the precious self. How stupid can you be I used to tell myself. Once again the problem whole of drinking is seen to be greater than the sum of its parts because the degradation of the physical and mental states feed each other. Here's another thing – people with liver problems as the result of drinking are more likely to have heart problems as well. The correlation between a longer lifespan and drastically cutting down is obvious but must be reiterated to ourselves whenever we have the hint of a pang once the path begins. Why alcohol causes myopathy is still only partly understood. It may be due to the malnutrition which occurs in drinkers because booze cuts the effectiveness of the body's ability to absorb some nutrients. A definite connection has been made with drink and vitamin D deficiency. A lack of vitamin D results in the body not being able to use other nutrients such as phosphorus in maintaining proper muscular cell function and metabolism, resulting in improper function or atrophy. When I learnt this I began to take a combined supplement containing vitamin D as well as calcium and magnesium to help my bone maintenance and muscle function. Living in the UK this is important in the case of vitamin D because our main source of it otherwise is sunlight. Enough said!

Supertiredness
Why do you feel totally washed out and knackered the day after drinking? Basically the quality of sleep you get is of dire

quality. Drinking alcohol can reduce the amount of Rapid Eye Movement (REM) sleep you get. This is why you feel drowsy the next day. I also found it much harder to concentrate. Monday mornings were the worst when I was almost zombie-like. The switch from weekends to the working week holds a certain degree of mental trauma for most except those who prefer work to non-work life. Even when I wasn't drinking there was always a degree of vegetableness about me on a Monday which was amplified when drinking. I'm amazed now that I held a slight irrational fear of Monday mornings even in jobs that I liked that put me at a disadvantage to others even before the week's bell had rung. Latent fears within us all are brought out and amplified by booze. Back to the sleep detriments of booze – although alcohol may help you to drop off faster it disrupts your sleep. During 'normal' sleep patterns (which did not return to me until five days after a drinking cycle had ended), you move between non-REM slow wave sleep about three quarters of the time and REM sleep for the other quarter. After a drinking day, you fall straight into deep non-REM sleep and the time in REM sleep is severely diminished. REM is the mentally restoring kind of sleep hence the feeling of supertiredness upon waking. More than this your body's efforts to metabolise alcohol takes you out of deep sleep and into so called Stage 1 non REM sleep, which counters the restorative efforts of the brain meaning that even if you kept asleep for eight hours nonstop (unlikely with a replete rectum) you still feel tired the next day. Alcohol also affects normal sleeping by causing excessive snoring – another reason I was banished by my wife to the spare room. I made the earth move alright but only by the violence of my log sawing. Because I started drinking early in the day I slept for a few hours at midday to 'freshen up' for the afternoon's tasks. This quite obviously messed up my night's sleep further because I had already had some and meant I would awake in the early hours and have an horrendous cycle of droppings off and awakenings until I got up. When I ended a drinking cycle for a few days after I felt extremely tired at midday as my body was conditioned for sleeping then. When you have embarked on the path and your sleep patterns start coming around to normality and you get eight hours including the proper period of REM – you really appreciate how important sleep is through how wonderful you feel and the sharpness of your waking thoughts. Mundus in claritate!

Alcohol & Weight Gain

I'm afraid whichever way you look at it body weight is the result of calories in > calories out. Well maybe not quite, it depends on the complexity of the food or drink too and your body's ability to digest it. You have little ability to digest bran flakes and absorb little of their calories before expelling the rest in the process that's best not mentioned. Alcohol's structure though is not so complex and is easily absorbed and the energy from it quickly made available by your liver. You certainly don't exercise while drinking (apart from bending the elbow) so the body stores the broken-down molecules eventually as fat. Anyone who's drank also knows booze increases appetite. Which of the following are you likely to eat after a session – quinoa salad or donner meat and chips? Not only do you eat more you eat rubbish. Leptin is a hormone that regulates appetite and decreases hunger. The level of leptin in the body decreases by half in a booze session. Also before the mega meals at the end of the session there is also the snacking during it. Which of the following are you likely to eat during a session – quinoa salad or crisps, toffee coated peanuts, pork scratchings and chocolate? The former for me… only kidding!

Alcohol contains a lot of calories – a can of 5% lager 215, a glass of wine 228. This means that without the excess eating of all the crappy fatty stuff, during a standard drinking day of my old cycles, a 16 canner, I would take in 3,440 extra calories or the best part of 1,000 over the recommended daily calorie intake for me – without even eating a bean. Drinking increases the amount of nasty subcutaneous fat which deposits itself in the abdominal area of the body. In men this is a cause of a beer belly and happens irrespective of age. If I hadn't been drinking the amount of sit ups I used to do would have given me a Mr Universe tum – but as it was they could only fight a losing battle with my beer gut. Also because of its propensity to increase the levels of the feminising hormone oestrogen, it can increase the chances of gyneacomastia or the infamous 'moobs' in men (oestrogen increase will also affect the breast size of women). If I hadn't been drinking the amount of press ups I used to do would have given me a Mr Universe chest – but as it was they could only fight a holding action with my moobies.

Alcohol and the Immune System

When you drink a lot of alcohol, it has many negative effects on your digestive system. It destroys epithelial cells in your intestines, making it harder to absorb many nutrients. It also severely disturbs your gut's microbiome, significantly altering the balance of healthy and unhealthy bacteria. As a result the way health gut microbes interact with the immune system is affected. Alcohol also disrupts the gut barrier, allowing more bacteria to pass into the blood. Some of these bacteria can cause inflammation of a liver already under siege from other effects of alcohol and can lead to new or further liver damage. I always drink my probiotic yoghurt every day now to bolster the morale of my microbes on which I used to inflict the most heinous war crimes. Alcohol also affects the respiratory system which can lead to increased risk of pneumonia, TB and acute respiratory distress syndrome. I have always had slight bronchitis for which I take the appropriate inhalers, and the couple of days after a drinking cycle would feel a definite tightening of my bellows. Because the protective qualities of the mucus is impaired in both the lungs and digestive tract, any disease contracted can become more severe.

Excessive drinking reduces the number and function of three important kinds of cells in your immune system: macrophages, T and C cells. Macrophages are the first line of defence against disease. They are the sanitation squad that consume anything that's not supposed to be there, including cancerous cells, and they sound the alarm if pathogens are present. T cells are antibodies to specific pathogens. They are the reason vaccines work and why you can't get certain diseases twice because your T cells already know how to eliminate the virus. B cells are white blood cells that produce cytokines to attack bacteria. When B and T cells are suppressed, your immune system is less efficient at identifying and killing invading pathogens. Regular heavy drinking is very bad news for your immune system – every time you drink heavily your immune system is knocked out. If you are then in a place where others can come into close proximity to you, your defences will be lowered when you are most exposed to bacteria and viruses.

Liver Cirrhosis

The big one. If you drink heavily you are putting yourself at risk from this – doesn't matter who you are. The really worrying thing is you may not have any symptoms during the early stages and keep merrily on. It causes the liver to become scarred and as it becomes more scarred and damaged only then may you feel early stage symptoms. These are feeling very tired and weak – the tiredness might be disguised by that attributable to poor sleep, due to the booze, but the weakness is a new thing. Other early stage symptoms are nausea (over and above that caused when your stomach is saying no more volume!), appetite loss and the losing of the sex drive – the latter would have been largely hidden from me as I was residing often in the spare room. All the above may be hidden in the other symptoms of alcohol abuse. But as the condition gets worse unequivocal signs appear. These can include jaundice (yellowing of the whites of the eyes and skin), vomiting blood, bleeding easily and a build up of fluid in the legs and stomach causing swelling. If you have any of these, see a doctor immediately. If your liver is severely scarred it can stop functioning and then a liver transplant is the only option. Scary – of course it is. I knew I was on course for this with a lashed rudder and engines stuck on full forward. I had to do something or that would have been it. Even I wasn't daft enough not to realise this. Some say you have to lose everything before you realise you have an alcohol problem. Losing everything is dying in my book – this serves to show the idiocy of that statement. No, you weigh everything and can see the downsides of drinking are now heavier in the balance than the upsides and decide to act.

CHAPTER FIVE

CHARTING YOUR IMPROVEMENT

It is very important to record all your data every step of the way on the path right from the start. This is so you can track the reduction in alcohol intake as it reduces toward zero. The tracking starts from your first PRD. It will aid your progress through the facts presented that will unequivocally show your improvement over time. Really get into this tracking – it's a real scientific dimension to your project that will aid you in shoring up the emotional aspects. It's not too onerous – it just involves recording the amount of units taken in a Planned Relapse Day and the day itself. The data used in the recording are governed by the Oaken Rules. It's always worth reminding ourselves of these:

First Oaken Rule: 'A PRD shall be no more than one day long'.
Second Oaken Rule: 'The time to the next PRD must be greater than it was to the last one'.
Third Oaken Rule: 'Plan only the next PRD'.

Three simple rules to a better life! To show that they are being adhered to we must collect and apply the stats. I'll say once and never again that this must be done honestly – self deception here will insidiously lead to ruin. Record everything faithfully. By running this as an objective project we get behind it even more fully. This next point is of supreme import. The strategy of the PRDs and the tactical weapons are designed to keep you on the path. Once I had embarked on the path, The Trigger was never again pulled and the Oaken Rules have never been broken – even though I was amongst the weakest of the weak. Nothing is 100% infallible however. If you stray, look at the picture of the uncorrupted you and ask yourself do you really want to do something about your drinking? Are the upsides for you still weightier on the balance? If the answer is no from that point you must plan the next PRD and follow the Oaken Rules. Mark down the day you transgressed along with the units you drank and include them in the analysis I am about to describe.

First of all we need to record a standard time period over which we can compare the number of PRDs and units taken from one to the next. For me this was 30 days. Everybody's pattern of PRDs will be different, but I think this is about right to start with. Your first PRD will be at the very beginning of your first 30-day period. Once you have taken the PRD record the number of units you drank as accurately as you possibly can to the nearest half unit. Remember this will be more or less difficult depending on the type of alcohol you had and if you watered it down. Come equipped to the PRD with your method of calculation and measurement of booze taken. Once you have hit on the measurement methodology it must be used consistently with all subsequent PRDs.

Divide the total number of units taken in a period with the number of PRDs in that period. Log all values in your dedicated notebook.

Once recorded, we must tabulate the data from the first 30 days. We will use this data to draw a simple graph of our progress. I will describe the process using MS Excel. It's very easy but it can be simply done in the old-fashioned way with graph paper if needs be. First we need a simple master data table. You can start the graph after two periods of 30 days but in the example I am using we'll assume six periods have passed. The values entered under the '30' column are for day 1 (when you took your first PRD) to day 30 inclusive, the values under the '60' column day 31 to day 60 inclusive etc. This is just an example to show the methodology – please don't use it as a template for your PRD plan! If you stray from the path add the day you transgressed to the number of PRDs in the relevant time period together with units drunk.

Master Data Table – example

	30	60	90	120	150	180
PRDs	7	3	3	2	2	1
Units per PRD	22	21	20	19	20	19

To show our progress tending towards zero it is best to arrange the data into a cumulative average for each period of 30 days. This is because otherwise there will be time periods with zeros in them followed by a time period where we take a PRD. To show our drinking going up by 100%

CHARTING YOUR IMPROVEMENT

for this period would be misleading – we need to represent our overall progress right from the start of our journey. Also notice the units per PRD. In the example the units per PRD actually increased from 120-150 days. Even though there was this blip the overall cumulate average number of units per PRD reduced (as we will see from the graph we produce). This is why we plot the cumulative averages at the end of each time period, it gives a better representative overall picture.

Making the Cumulative Average Table is dead easy. Start by copying the first pair of values (of the '30' days column) from the Master Data Table into the '30' column of the new table – the Cumulative Average Table (shown below). Then add the PRDs in the '30' and '60' columns together, divide by two and enter this number under the '60' column of the new table. Of course with Excel you can put in a simple formula to achieve this, linking the two columns together – but you don't have to. Then add the number of PRDs in the '30', '60' and '90' columns together, divide by three and enter the number under the '90' column in the new table. Carry on in this vein until the 'PRD Cum Av' row is filled in the new table. If there is zero in a time period do exactly the same thing – still 'add' it to the previous values and as always divide by the new total number of time periods elapsed. Good for you for the zero by the way! Repeat with exactly the same method for the Cum Av Units per PRD row. Using the data from the Master Data Table above, the following table is produced:

Cumulative Average Table

	30	60	90	120	150	180
Cum Av PRDs	7.0	5.0	4.3	3.8	3.4	3.0
Cum Av Units per PRD	22.0	21.5	21.0	20.5	20.4	20.2

Make sure in this table the value in the two rows are shown to one decimal point. To do this in Excel highlight the relevant numbers and right click. Select 'Format Cells' from the menu. Then select 'Number' from the list on the left-hand side of this menu. Finally set 'Decimal places' to 1.

Now it's time to produce the graph. Do this in the following steps:

1. Highlight the entire Cumulative Average Table (including the empty cell at top left to complete the rectangle).
2. On the tool bar select 'Insert'. A number of chart types will appear below the tool bar.
3. Select 'Line'. A number of different types of line graph appear.
4. Hover your cursor over each – the description of the graph will be displayed.
5. Click on the 'Line with Markers' option. Et voilà! The following graph appears.

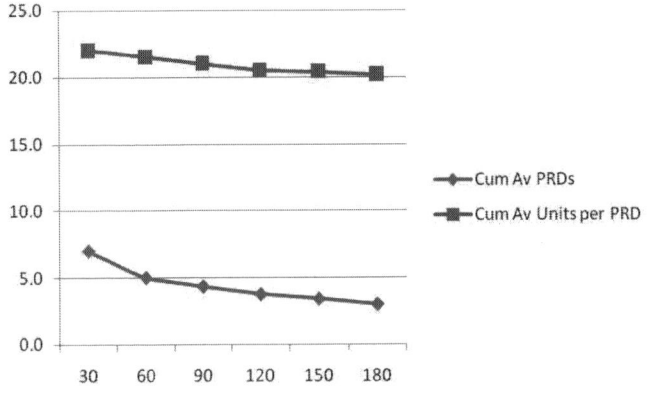

This graph is good to go as it is – the one shown is the one produced out of the box as it were. You can drag it around your Excel sheet to the position you wish. You can also jazz up its appearance by right clicking within the chart either in the Chart Area, the Plot Area, The Legend or either of the two Axes. The message of the chart will be unaltered but you can customise its looks by selecting the 'Format' options at the bottom of the menus that come up.

To extend the graph after each time period update the Master Data Table and Cumulative Average Table on the spreadsheet. Within the graph right click and select 'Select Data'. A pop up box appears. Highlight the whole of the Cumulative Average Table including the new values and click 'ok' on the pop up box. The graph lines will extend to the latest period.

You can of course produce two graphs one for Cum Av PRDs and one for Cum Av Units per PRD. Because each graph will be optimally scaled your improvements from time period to time period will look more apparent. I prefer showing both graphs on the same axes however – I like to see all my improvements in one hit. The effect of the whole is greater for me.

If the Oaken Rules are followed neither graph can turn upwards. The lower graph will tend towards zero – you can actually see what this means now! As time goes by and the numbers get lower you may wish to record over longer time periods – no point keep re-entering '0' in the PRDs row of the Master Data Table. So you might use 90 days as your time period. Then add together the first three sets of data from the Master Data Table, the second lot of three sets etc until you have a new 90 day table. It's important to include all the information right from the first PRD because this is the reference point from which your progress is measured. Recalculate the values in the Cumulative Average Table and redraw the graph.

Whichever method you use, an excel sheet, or a notebook laid out with graph paper – it should be very precious to you. Guard the data well, ensure it is backed up and transferred across to a new computer. Blow the graph up and print it off and stick it up on the wall if this works for you in an understated place though, not gilt framed over the fireplace! Just watch out for the effects of various kinds of adhesive on your wallpaper when you pull it off to hang the updated version. I've been there and the rip was met with Germanic admonishment.

CHAPTER SIX

CHANGES – THE NEXT STEPS ON THE PATH

How do you change when following the path? How did I change? How do your thoughts and feelings change after the first PRD and leading into subsequent ones? It's important to expect to feel better. The further you are removed from the destructive drink cycles the feeling of addiction, dependence and wanting will correspondingly fade. It helps to keep the thought when pangs do occur that to hanker after that you are being saved from is daft. I guarantee though after the first Recovery Day you will feel really good and positive and ready to strive forward – the earliness of the path's progress being its strength at this point. Allow yourself to feel good and don't start looking for problems that aren't there when you do feel good. We have discussed the tactical weapons that can be deployed if necessary. You will have written these down sometime in the period of deciding to do something about your drinking and the first PRD. You will have cut them to fit your personal cloth. They are ready and waiting to go if required. Have them at the tips of your fingers. They are categorised as countermeasures to thoughts you may have trying to justify a drink outside of the PRDs, those to deal with situations where you will be exposed to temptation and those that use practical steps to ensure you physically can't drink. I'll show how I needed to deploy some of mine. Overarching the whole path is the strategy of the PRDs. This is the stout staff that supports you on the steps of the path – which is required less as your own two legs become stronger. I repeat expect to feel better – all is in your favour now.

On the first RD after the first PRD or on the day after (a Standard Day) it's time to plan your next PRD. Remember the Third Oaken Rule – Only plan the next PRD. You can't plan more because you don't know how you will feel post your re-evaluation of the effects of drink on you after the next. You may after this one not want to plan another for a significant length of time. Personally, I planned my second PRD to take place nine days after the first. It felt about right and my wife would be away on that Sunday and on the Monday I knew I had a planned dental appointment which my work knew about. I had played up with work the fact that I may be whooshy on that day because I never react well to the pain jab – which they were fine with. There was a modicum of truth in this – but I made sure I did thoroughly cover myself to ensure no ill effects of a professional or personal nature ensued from the PRD. There was some deception but minimised through thorough planning that is vital to our preparation for PRDs. I knew now I was getting better and stronger through following this path. Work would also benefit even in the short term as I felt my confidence returning which is vital to my performance. As the PRDs became less as they must the subterfuge would lessen anyway. As long as no family or work colleagues are being compromised or really disadvantaged by your PRD and RD it's OK – if they would be choose another day. Don't arouse other suspicions such as the possibility you've taken a fancy woman, or fancy man for that matter – plan judiciously and cover yourself totally. Within the next nine days were some of the best I'd had in many a moon. The first SD though after the RD following that first PRD was quite tough but I had expected that it might be. It was a Sunday (you'll remember I chose Friday for my first PRD). I was wrong footed almost straight away when I cut open the bag of haylage for the horse first thing in the morning. As I've recounted, suddenly I was in a brewery and got a powerful pang. I had to wait it out. I was at the start of something big, to fail now over such a trifle would be very bad for me – to be sunk by hitting a pooberg so soon. My imp was blathering on but I faced down the danger. I marked the experience and wrote it down under my list of Situational Tactical Weapons. The specific countermeasure was to be aware of this each morning. By being ready for it subsequently I never experienced this feeling in the stable again. The night before I had written down some of the tasks that I would plan to carry out on that Sunday – my first ever Standard Day. This was done with no great detail or indeed precision, it being my first RD I was scatterbrained to say the least, but it was required to be done and I was glad now I had done it. I simply did not want to run out of ideas for things to do and have hours of brooding aimlessness stretching out. I didn't do all the tasks and none of them very well but was very glad that the piece of paper gave me options, so I didn't have to think about planning them at the time. It really was the Creeping Barrage strategy at its most base and functional. After feeding the horse I went to the gym and had a right good session – achieving my baseline effort which always makes me feel good in myself. In the past, when I had completed my exercise in this way, The Trigger was apt to be pulled in the shower afterwards as my imp would yell 'reward time!' This time I was ready for it – it was a tactical situation I had planned for and its knowledge had become a weapon against it. I was also ready to do what I felt like when I felt like – not to carry out the tasks of a 'regular' Sunday in their regular order. Knowing I could do what I felt like in any order was of paramount use to me that day and after the haylage incident I honestly did not feel again like a drink all day. I sent my imp to a specially constructed limbo with trials as of Tartarus (he's no friend of mine), from which he knackerdly stirs ever less.

Anyway, these are the things I did during the rest of the day. There was no discernable plan that day, I just did what I felt like at the time. Not that I was charging around in a state of utter distraction I wasn't, but I did feel at times that a squad of soldier ants had made camp in my boxers. On returning from the gym before leaving the car I counted the Euro coins in a bag I kept them in because we had a trip to Belgium planned through the tunnel. Known as 'pooros', these coins are for the payment required to get through the turnstiles to gain access to loos in Belgian service stations in case of being taken short on the road. Then on an impulse I took off in the car again without getting out remembering a light bulb had failed in the house the previous night and needed replacing. After a successful purchasing trip I returned to the house to replace it. Question – how many people starting upon the path does it take to change a light bulb on a SD after the RD after the first PRD? None! – they all get electrocuted before they can do it due to the absent mindedness inherent in the Creeping Barrage. Bit of a clunky 'joke' but it does bring to the fore a pertinent point – in the early days where Creeping Barrages are necessarily employed, don't choose to do things where life and death stuff may happen. Obviously drink driving – but this is always a red line where you can harm others – what I mean here is don't take on tasks where your absent mindedness can put you or others in peril. This is only for a short while – it soon gets better and you will be able to use on these days your full range of cognitive and motor functions without distraction. Next, I replaced a bare toilet roll with a fresh one – marvelling at how long it had lasted compared to more booze induced squelchy times. Once again absentmindedness struck – perspiring through the exertion of changing the bulb and roll, I reached for a wipe protruding out of its pack. Not paying attention, I wiped my face with a floor cleaning wipe, realising when I spotted with horror the pack of facial wipes in close proximity. As the solution of the wipe bit into that morning's razor burns I re-learnt the need to pay greater heed to what I was doing through the teachings of perfect agony. My wife thought it humorous, me about as funny as myxomatosis in Malta.

Next, I saw a pin and surreptitiously threw it on the floor, 'saw it' and picked it up. This is a daily ritual of mine – I buy pins in boxes of 500 in order to get a regular stream of good luck. I have to say from this point onwards on the path it worked better and better. I went upstairs to rehang my favourite print on the wall now it had come back from the framers: *The Fight Between Carnival and Lent* by Bruegel and went back down. I played *At the Castle Gate* by Sibelius on YouTube. Now it was still only eleven and I suddenly felt the time weighing on me. We have a big wall clock in the kitchen with a deep resounding tick. I thought 'blimey, aren't seconds long?' as I bit my nails. I felt I was treading water in the middle of Panthalassa – dry land so far away and saw the danger. I went out to the garden and attended to the Carolina Reaper chillies I was growing in a mini greenhouse. Some time back I had thought of growing these as a Physical Tactical Weapon to chew one down in an extreme emergency – after all you can't drink with an inflamed oesophagus but dismissed this as barking. I still continued growing them though as I like to make really hot curries. While watering them I sang the Cuckoo Song nearly all the way through and then key verses of old humorous Lancashire monologues according to my like that my father used to relate. After this, still being outside I fed my grey squirrels that live in the horse chestnut trees. I pondered the fact that they get an almost universal bad rap especially in the UK – actually I rather do like them not least because they wind up some people with too much time on their hands. You know what they say – 'they've come in displacing our English Reds.' They are just doing what they do it's the way nature works. Grey's haven't got some sinister Machiavellian agenda of conquest to personally antagonise them. These people assume that a squirrel's world view is the same as ours. They assume the Greys have a working knowledge of our county lines. So they say things like 'the Greys are about to move north from their base in the Home Counties' as though the squirrels are saying amongst themselves: 'right chaps we've secured Berkshire time to move on Oxfordshire.' Anyway this is my view on the matter on which I pondered. It killed time.

After this feeling much happier and safer I went for a walk with my wife and the dog. We live in an area where flint pieces lie on the ground and I spotted a good big sharp piece on the walk. When I got home I decided to start chipping it with another stone to fashion a Neolithic knife which I did distractedly. After my wife had finished bandaging my hand I was down to the last couple of hours of potential danger. I watched the first half of *Duck Soup* (Marx Brothers) I'd taped a few days back. Then I read two chapters of *The Way We Live Now* by Anthony Trollope. Reading such as this has always had the effect of pouring oil on my waters. I finished with half an hour to go. I would usually prefer to drink a flagon of sarin infused novochok than do what I did next but found myself sitting in front of my computer... I went on a Sci-Fi blog site thing and vented my spleen on the first thing I could think of that got my goat's craw. I wrote along the lines of, 'You know what I don't get. After all these years why can't Starfleet Command invent a cloaking device? I mean every other bugger's had them for bloody ages'. Unutterably sad yes to make oneself murderously irksome over such an issue, but it got me through most of my last minutes. My final act to fill the last five minutes to 17:00 was to change the password on my computer EVEN THOUGH I had been prompted that morning that I had fourteen days in which to do so. I vowed that before the next password change I would be operating at the best level I could in mind and body. That evening I felt fantastic – actually looking forward to work the next day.

Nevertheless, I remembered The Trigger being fired more on Monday mornings than any other time when working from home and so gave my wallet and enclosed credit and debit cards to my wife and slept all the better for it.

On Monday morning I felt fresh and raring to go. I decided to do a weight check. After the day's initial ablutions, I got on the bathroom scales and the readout was another incentive to continue what I'd begun in consigning the calories of booze to the pedal bin. I always rather disingenuously take a pound off whatever the scales say. So that morning the scales read 16st and I said to myself I'm 15st 13 pounds, because there's probably a pound still in there somewhere I haven't quite managed to get rid of yet this morning. Oh really! Where's it hiding? In which part of the colon/bowel apparatus has it secreted itself? Try eating a pound bag of sugar and pretending you don't know about it. But I still felt pretty good about myself as I turned on the computer. I attacked work even though I was working from home that day and was actually *proactive* – I went looking for tasks to do and really engaged with the wider team to get all the updates possible so I was the one that was armed with all the reports, stats and inside information for the day's internal and customer calls. There are moments where I found myself brooding throughout the day, but I was able to recognise what was happening and snap myself out of it. Over the next few days, I was required to think about the next PRD about three or four times just to shore me up. These instances were nearly always driven by certain instances of work pressure. The thought of the PRD stopped me drinking when in the past when I would have drunk no question. On one morning I deployed this weapon – if I eat heavily, I don't feel like drinking, needed because when out walking the dog I felt a bit vulnerable. I used to love porridge before it became trendy and irritating and made a big batch of it when I got back to the house – the proper plain oats of my youth made on a hob with the merest trace of treacle for sweetness – not one of those microwave pots of flavoured parody. I enjoyed it hugely and it achieved the objective it was intended to gain. Later I had a diet coke and thought about how the texture of its fizzyness is similar to beer yet I'm still clear headed after drinking it. For the first time in a very long time I liked myself properly, through sobriety, not through drunkenness that engenders only phoney self-adulation.

During the period to my second PRD I made myself think back to times in the past when The Trigger had been pulled. Do the same exercise yourself, really rationalise the past workings of The Trigger. By ring fencing the concept and remembering some specific instances the conditions for its being pulled again were undermined. Even if it was still there somewhere lurking this remembrance of instances past together with the promise of the next PRD and the tactical weapons ready and waiting if required kept it from being pulled. There were times though leading to the second PRD when the danger was almost critical and I could really have done with a medium term important event to focus on and prepare for. Perhaps I should have manufactured one to focus on.

The first few days after the first PRD, I was also very careful about how I ate before bedtime. I didn't eat for four hours before turning in and did not choose heavy carbohydrates for tea ('tea' from where I originate is most people's 'dinner' – 'dinner' being most's 'lunch'). Even without booze I know that a heavy meal before bedtime makes me broody upon waking even if I sleep all the night though. Don't get me wrong the thoughts I had were not of the order of destructiveness and perfect anguish of when I had been drinking but could be detrimental to my well-being and diminish the feeling of constant upward improvement I was certainly experiencing. So not to start ruminating like a Friesian as soon as my eyes opened, I was careful about how, when and what I ate as my last meal of the day. I took my vitamin supplements but got a bit over exuberant. I had bought a big pack of chewable vitamin C of which you are only supposed to take one a day. But I found them very nice and once I had one I couldn't stop treating them like premium midget gems. I got a bad stomach and learnt a lesson – moderation in all things you put inside you at this time and do not exceed the recommended dose.

So in the period between the first and second PRD I deployed a fair few tactical weapons of my arsenal but the message I would really like to get across is despite some bumpy moments they worked and within the nine days was a story of continuous improvement in my well-being, performance and happiness of my wife, work colleagues and in general the world to which I turned my outward face.

The day before my second PRD I felt alternately guilt and anticipation. The guilt was borne of the anticipation of course and consisted of mainly 'should I be taking this path instead of stopping altogether?' I really did know however, that the thought of tomorrow's event had got me through some dodgy times in the past nine days and if it were not for knowledge of the PRD I might well have succumbed. If I had been a different person, I might have been in a position to defer the PRD. As we are discussing the realpolitik of booze, warts and all, it's best I highlight the danger of deferment so early on the path. I do this to ensure you stick to the Oaken Rules. Remember the Second Oaken Rule: The time to the next PRD must be greater than it was to the last one. To put it bluntly by deferring it at this early stage you may find the time to the subsequent one is too long. So early on in the PRD programme consider deferment carefully. Later you will have the will and confidence to defer as you wish.

I was able to note that my anticipation levels were nothing like as strong as before my first PRD. On the day I followed the guideline of only buying the drink on the day itself. I had enough of last night's sausage casserole left for the herculean meal, so didn't buy much food except crisps and some dry roasted peanuts. I had a consideration about my weight because my health and weight loss programme was concurrently running and I didn't want to nause it up completely through this day. I felt a hint of pride in myself that I had made the concession of not buying too many snacks and no choccy at all this time. I had made it because my weight loss was more important than pure hedonism even for one day. But we should not hold back on PRDs if we don't want to especially with the drink bit. To feel 'unfulfilled' through drink on a PRD is dangerous in that it could lead to drinking the next day in order to feel fulfilled and this would break the First Oaken Rule. This is the realpolitik of the situation. The most effective check on the amount of alcohol taken on a PRD is its recording. This has been so powerful with me. As time went on I really couldn't wait to update my graphs to see the variation in their trends from the last PRD and overall – from when the path was first joined. It is so important therefore that you record faithfully and consistently the units you took on the PRD to the half unit. For me I found I drank less and less on subsequent PRDs anyway as my body simply couldn't take the previous volumes. There are checks that you will have therefore on the amount you drink on a PRD even though you are not explicitly limiting yourself. After you have recorded your data and plotted the new graph extension after a PRD you may see a downward turn on the lower graph which, by itself, may lead to a half a unit or more reduction during the next PRD just to keep that ol' line going down.

I actually went to the gym first on the morning of my second PRD. I wanted to get something else out of the day and have a good workout. I felt good afterwards but even so it was immediately afterwards that I visited the supermarket to stock up. Apart from the 'food' items related above, from the magazine sections I bought the adult comic I still like after all these years, and a light hearted current affairs bi weekly. As I was taking the PRD at home I would have easy access to the internet and so be able to get on all sorts of sites to pass the day. I got some cans, paused before paying and turned to get some more because the amount could be a little light. When I got home I mentally shut up shop and pulled the first ring. I won't pretend I didn't like the first few. I tried to make myself feel bad in that I was boozing just for boozing's sake and I wasn't moving any of my personal projects forward within this free day. I could have moved forward the short story I was having a go at etc. In this I was only partially successful. But the day certainly didn't have as much going for it funwise as the first PRD. This may have been because it was a cloudy day with interminable drizzle which imparted melancholy. Trying to force remorse into myself ceased at the start of the la la phase. I flicked through the current affairs magazine, alighting on only the funny sections not those of serious debate. I read the comic from cover to cover. I then played my usual YouTube songs from my favourite bands. After a while of this I had nothing else to do so I flicked around with the telly's remote to find something. Nothing really stuck – I alighted on some programmes, spending about a minute on each, before I switched back to the top of the menu of 'all channels' and started to flick through each page again. I stood up and knocked over a vase on my way to the loo. This took the edge off the joy – it would need a fair dose of brass for me to replace it and my wife would probably think that I had been drinking which would require a rebuttal I hadn't planned for. I grudgingly swept up the bits, the task intruding on the purity of my pleasure. A few weeks later a stray piece would strike my heel and leave me unable to walk proper for three days. I had drunk about as much as this point in my first PRD when I re-heated the sausage casserole at about 13:00 – the volume of which I supplemented by stirring in a catering tin of new potatoes. I wolfed it and went to bed. After two hours when I awoke, my feelings compared to the last PRD were diminished. I felt mentally empty – it was mid afternoon and I had nothing to do for the rest of the day. I started flicking through the remote channels again finding only emptiness. I even tried the titillation, to my deserved shame, of alighting on the ten minute freeviews in the channels of the 'Adult' menu. Because it was daytime there wasn't a lot to see as apparel was to the fore so after a bit of shamethrill gave up. Sorry – case of idle hands doing the Devil's work, but the joke was on him because I would be snoring after 22:00 when it really ramps up. Was ever an afternoon wasted in a more inane way? I did feel its inaneness. My wife called at 17:00 and I sounded normal as though I hadn't drunk anything. The joy of the early day had utterly disappeared and my mind was devoid of any of the exuberance of booze which was reflected in my voice. It showed me that the whole drink thing is a state of mind as much as narcotic effect. She said how miserable I sounded, and I confirmed this but thought it unnecessary right now to trouble her of knowledge of the vase. After the call, because they were there like Everest, I recommenced the cans. I was bloated and every swallow increased the bloatedness and the acidity in my stomach was causing heartburn so I did what I always used to and switched from the pint pot to a tiny liqueur glass from which I sipped small but often. In this way I got through four more cans and a bag of peanuts before my body really said enough. I threw away the remaining cans down the sink and turned in for the night.

I awoke in the small hours as usual and my head felt like the battle of Stamford Bridge. This was unusual for me, usually I didn't get headaches from my old drinking sessions but did I ever now. I went to get some paracetamol and after taking it my liver felt like it was about to do an Alien out of my chest. I lay awake thinking how rotten I was going to feel for a couple of days afterwards. I felt like I was back to square one. I had a turn of cramp and could feel a slight soreness on the instep of my left food – a pretext to its swelling. And I had put so much into my training too. Back to bloody square one, why did you do it? Bloody lame again, sodding heck! My mouth was as dry as a lime basket and when I got up to get water and put weight on my foot the proto pain confirmed that I would be hobbling AGAIN for at least five days. That's put the tin hat on drinking for me I thought. Back in bed I thought this is a complete bloody waste of life – dead time. Like the period between paying for your goods at Argos and being told to go to your collection point please. I got up and counted the cans – one less than last time – one little victory. I wrote the number of units down in my notebook. After movements had ceased bowelside I got on the scales with dread. The readout showed I had put on four pounds since the day before – I knew this might be temporarily high due to water retention etc… but four pounds! – and hobbling around to bloody boot so no gym visits to get it off quick. Perfect unadulterated anguish. Pon Farr with bells on.

On this Recovery Day I reflected on my feelings about the previous day. The first was it had set me back, not only from my exercise and weight loss initiatives that had been progressing quite nicely, but also from my ways of thinking. In the couple of days leading to the PRD I had felt unfettered in my thinking. But it was more that this – I had been able to experience joy without the narcotic and knew them to be true joys. The joys I experienced were through the big things, seeing my wife happy because I wasn't boozing and because I was acting like I was when courting and during early marriage (when I never drank on days in which we had contact) and doing a decent job at work. But also in the little things, such as the progress of my growing potato crop or the blackbirds in the laurel hedge. It was such little things which, when drinking, I would appreciate them then immediately feel the requirement to drink to maximise the experience. In the days leading to my second PRD I didn't have the need for this amplification – my unaltered senses were enough. Now on this RD I knew if not quite back to the square one, I felt I'd gone down the big snake on square ninety nine. I was afraid again, my confidence tank empty and I didn't feel tough anymore like I had the day before the PRD, tough enough to take on any comer especially *them* who had done me wrong when I had been vulnerable in the state I had been when drinking who I sorely wanted to redeem myself with if not settle some accounts. I never said I was perfect! Luckily the RD had been planned so there were no real interactions with *them* or indeed anyone else where mental performance or resilience of any degree was required. I only felt like a drink once that day but it was powerful. It was in the morning after all my e-mails had been checked and replied to. I got the feeling after I had completed the last e-mail. It wasn't helped by the fact that I had not washed the small liqueur glass I had used the evening before. Now, just prior to rinsing it, I caught a whiff of stale beer. Lesson learnt – get rid of all sights and smells of drink before you turn in on the night of the PRD so you don't get temptations the next day through simple oversights like this. This time the feeling of wanting a drink was overwhelmed quickly. I sat myself down and said, 'no way'. Although I didn't consciously itemise the elements behind the 'no way' they were a combination of: you must keep to the path now you've begun; the Oaken Rules are sacrosanct; imagine the untold wretchedness you would suffer writhing in bed tomorrow morning; remember how good you felt a couple of days ago; it's not as though you can never ever drink again. Once I'd had this moment of danger I was OK for the day and got better and better as it progressed. I used the Creeping Barrage technique but felt that I could concentrate much better than any other day I could remember after a serious skinful. The previous day's events really did feel like getting drunk for drunk's sake and I had really buggered myself up because of it. Now I felt a determination that I hadn't felt before so soon after a drinking session to right myself double quick and continue on the path. I would have been content to just hold the line so it was great to sally forth. The one day of drinking hadn't troubled me to a really critical degree, therefore, because it was just one day. Two days I know would have led to three and then back to the old cycles when the wheels of my life would fall off again. I was not that daft. I updated my table in the afternoon and plotted my graphs. I had actually drunk two units less in my second PRD compared to the first. Both lines were nicely turned down therefore which gave me a good shot in the arm. Compare this feeling to other days past after a big drink when I would sink in a slough of self pity and despair, not to mention despond, leading to a feeling of almost intolerable wretchedness or going straight back onto the can. I strode forward. I wasn't going to urinate on my french fries. It wasn't easy and I was not free of booze baggage that day but it was a big improvement, even from my state on the first Recovery Day. I hadn't figured on my foot swelling, that was a real downer, but at least it made me throw myself into designing another exercise set that would keep me going until I could use it again. I also designed my diet over the next days to quickly be rid of the extra weight generated by the day before. It really brought open to me how my health, diet and fitness had improved over the last week ere the setback and how important these programmes were in supporting me on the overall path. I felt that day I could actually think and put two and two together. In the past on the first dry day after one of my old drinking cycles, I would write off even attempting anything cognitive because my mind would be so fogged up. Think of it – whole days out of your limited precious lifespan, where you give up using that which took so long to evolve. For the first time on a day after drink, I actually tried to use my mind to the best of my ability. I extended my short story by a couple of paragraphs. I would of course check it tomorrow to see if it passed muster after a non alcohol addled night's sleep. Nothing much, but the first time I could remember when I had not been so distracted or plain lazy the day after booze to trust my head to work at any decent level. I was toughening up even on the first day after a drink. I wouldn't say I was viagra hard but semi was good on this day. Time had slowed calmly through the day and I had made use of it.

So I had done two PRDs and RDs and could demonstrate progress to myself both through the stats and my base instinct which informed me I was making progress and feeling different and better than I had. I knew my instincts to be correct because I was following a programme that was working for me and I was judging myself against the adherence to that programme and the following of the Oaken Rules. I found myself not thinking about booze for ever longer periods and when I did it didn't bother me or I defaulted to the safety valve of the next PRD. So many times in the past after a couple of weeks of drinking I had convinced myself that all was going real well and I was set for life. The yawning finality of never again having a drink, ever to infinity plus one would present itself though eventually and once it had I would feel like a drink. I would beat it down, suppress the feeling and be fine again with my resolve redoubled. Then out of the blue The Trigger would be pulled and hey ho. Now I was building fortitude without forcing it and with reinforced concrete foundations. Now I knew I wasn't lying to myself about my getting better sticking, before I always suspected I might be. I planned the third PRD for three weeks hence. My firm at the time gave three days as holiday per year that you could use for charitable work or any endeavour you wished to pursue to learn a new skill. It was very generous and partly made up for the fact the regular amount of days leave was rather rubbish. Bit naughty that I should take such a day as a PRD – but it was on a Friday and hey, it this wasn't self improvement I don't know what was! Remember deception is necessary, but controlled deception that doesn't cause harm to others. Also on the second SD after my second PRD a medium term goal appeared on the horizon – a job interview in two weeks. I immediately labelled it as a Tactical Weapon and deployed it. I also thought through whether I should still take the PRD. I remembered however that the timings for the PRD should be arbitrary and not determined by other events as far as possible. Obviously though I didn't want to have an interview for at least three days after the PRD. This is a bone fide example of when to take the PRD timing into consideration because of another event. The PRD day as originally planned still fitted. You will know the events where you have to juggle slightly the days of your PRDs when they come up in between the time you plan the PRD and the day it's due to happen. Don't get into the habit of chopping and changing for events that don't really warrant it though. You will have originally chosen and planned a day where you can carry it out under safe conditions where your tracks can be covered. Moving it means you'll either bring it forward thereby jeopardising the Second Oaken Rule or push it out meaning the PRD may be too far into the future for your needs. Either way you'll get into an awful tizz before you know it – don't experience undue stress on this account. Once a PRD is in the diary do your level best to stick to it. You may defer it, but only because you feel in such a great place boozewise that you do not need or want it. This will be more likely when you have taken a few of them and have the first furlongs of the path in the bank.

I can tell you that it does get an awful lot easier as the path progresses. In the time after the second PRD my whole outlook began to change – thinking about drink was still there but with a greatly diminished effect. Booze just seemed to lose its relevance, its sting. Remember our analogy with gravity? As you get farther from the source the effect diminishes by the square of the distance from it? Well the pull also depends on the mass of the source in the first place. The moment I stopped one of my old drinking cycles, I began moving slowly away from a supermassive black hole and its effect was felt strongly even days after going on the wagon. Now on this path the islands of PRDs are more akin to a much lighter object like a star of just a solar mass in comparison – the effect of booze drops off quickly in the time after each. There will come a time when you see that even the comfort blanket of the next PRD is required less and less and you can plan it further out and when you have reached it, defer it without hardly any afterthought because drink means so little to you. Back to the story of my journey on the path. The gap between the second and third PRDs went easy, certainly because I had the medium term goal of the interview but I know it would have been easy anyway because I was now able to deal with time much better. I wasn't rushing towards five o' clock as an end in itself for the day. I was able to live for the moment, unselfconsciously, without wanting the moment to be remembered straight after to the max with booze. As it happened I failed the interview. I really wanted to get through to the next stage of the firm's hiring process because to be truthful I was too damaged within the job I had at the time for it to have a future. The old cycles of booze had holed me below the waterline before I started on the path and although things had been pulled back since, it was too high profile a role and there had been too many senior people who had been inconvenienced by my poor performance for me to survive long term. I'd relieved myself on my crinkle cuts there. Instead of drinking off the disappointment though I resolved, without even pondering on it, to show them all and kept on applying for roles straight after – this contrasted with previous failed interviews where a week disappeared in boozy introspection before I started the search again. After failing this interview, weighing the situation I was in with my current job, I actually wasn't far off being up defecation creek if not with paddle lost then with a bent oar. But this time instead of thinking I wish I could get back at *them*, I looked forward not back. My penchant for self pity and wounded pride that had increased in the last couple of decades, so I could hardly recognise my college self, was waning fast. I knew I had been a bad boy in the past and deserved a bi-cheek caning but I wasn't brooding on my inadequacies anymore but marshalling all my powers such as they were to go forward. My foot problem cleared up and I was able to restart my full exercise plan again. I was placing full faith in myself justified because I knew I was creating the optimal conditions to perform at my best because of my exercise, my diet, my supplements and especially because the number of units I was drinking was diminishing downwards, ever downwards as the time periods progressed. The third PRD was kept not deferred. The day panned out as usual – glug, YouTube, read, eat, sleep, glug, turn in for the night. In the early hours of the morning I awoke but I was armed and ready not to fall into the remorse pit of the past. I informed myself that my lousy feelings were due to chemical imbalances in my brain caused by the booze. My main feeling was that the previous day had been a waste. I remember feeling some joy at the first few glugs. It did feel a bit forced though at the time, I recalled, but the joy was still there I acknowledged. I remembered reading another chapter of the novel and how much less fun it was then when I was reading it sober. It wasn't just that my mind couldn't figure out and dissect the more complex passages or those inherent in the past style of the Victorian novel, it was that I couldn't be bothered doing anything that required deeper though and after seeing the chapter out I reverted to reading about famous battles on the internet. I would reread the chapter on the RD and it was as though I was reading it anew – nothing had sunk in. This wasn't Mr Trollope's fault – I expect he never intended for anyone to read his work bladdered. The whole PRD did not feel like an event as much as the previous two had. I was glad to be shot of it and get back to my life. Also I did mark that I had poured a fair amount of brass down the sink at evening's end which grated somewhat. When I did the stats I was again fair pleased about the course of the graphs although surprised to find I had drunk only half a unit less than last time. On the first SD this time I carried on with life without losing a step or at least without looking too much over my shoulder. The

PRD had taken a day out, the PRD itself, and a RD where I was not at my best but still able to function reasonably well. On balance I thought the PRD had been necessary. But this time I was confident enough to plan the next one quite a bit further out. It must be said though that if I had planned the fourth one for one day longer than the time between two and three – that would have been perfectly OK.

Before number four there were evenings where I gave my wallet to my wife for insurance. These were when rain had been forecast for the day after and very little was planned. I also put on a bit of weight which could be traced back to too much ice cream which I moderated when I realised what was causing it. A good balanced diet is of course always a good idea, but you should have fun also via what you eat – don't make yourself too miserable through diet especially early on the path. The greatest new thing I realised leading to the fourth PRD was I wasn't considering every single task before doing it I just did it. In the past I would walk past the bloody washing up all day almost not knowing how to start it, over thinking it instead of just up and doing it. That was all gone now. The biggest issue I had was that I was due to meet with the group of university friends I have already mentioned. The timing meant it just passed not contravening The Second Oaken Rule for my fourth PRD. I considered carefully whether to treat it as a PRD. The PRDs up to this point had got progressively easier. By easier I mean the days themselves went more or less the same, but the relevance of drink to me was diminishing after each one – they were becoming more of an inconvenience. In short they were doing what they were designed to do. I decided on this occasion I would rather treat the day as a PRD because it did fit with the

First Oaken Rule and that I still did not have the confidence not to drink when meeting them and did not want to cancel. As reported earlier the day went well enough. I kept track of the units I was drinking and drank a unit more than my last PRD. I used to drink at least 1.5 pints to everyone else's one so just by keeping track with the rest I found I was in no danger of making the lower graph go up, although my friends wanted to know 'what was wrong with me.' I thought again ashamedly why I was so different when drinking with friends (jollification itself) compared to my attitude to my wife when I had been drinking at home. In the latter case it was resentment at her prohibition of my drinking and of being caught. This did not excuse my reprehensible behaviour though in the ferocity of the backlash arguments I instigated. If you have a full social calendar and are used to socialising with others in places where drink is present it could be more difficult not to be tempted. Apart from the special case of drinking with this particular set of friends I can observe others drinking without any pangs and in fact revel in my sobriety compared to theirs. If you find temptation in these circumstances more difficult remember the Situation Tactical Weapon of preparing for them – how you will react when confronted by the drink and the questions and ribbing of peers concerning why you are not joining them. This fourth PRD with the boys was not much use as a PRD but at least I hadn't broken the First Oaken Rule. The RD afterwards was not pleasant. When two of them had a hair of the dog in the morning before we said our goodbyes – I had a litter of kittens but didn't join them. In this I had demonstrated to myself how far I had come although felt wretched at the time. I didn't want to feel that way again. When we met up ten months later I didn't drink at all. I had told them I wouldn't in good time. After their incredulity they accepted it. During that meeting I experienced a different kind of enjoyment but of the same level nonetheless. I had materially changed. By that time it was of no consequence to me to bat away the 'oh go on have just one!' requests. In fact after that fourth PRD with the boys I never again used a social occasion as a PRD.

So these were my first four PRDs. I have given them a fair amount of detail here because it will be useful for you to cross reference your experiences with mine and be ready for similar forces that surprised me and nearly deviated me from the path. During the time period encompassing the first four I felt continuous improvement in my health and mental performance and a reduction in all the negative aspects of addiction – cravings, brooding, sullenness, anxiety, inability to concentrate etc. The fourth as mentioned was a blip in my healing but I didn't break the Oaken Rules and so was able to easily get back on track the first Standard Day after it. I went into depth about the day out with the boys because it is part of the realpolitik of choosing the path – you have to be aware of all the dangers ahead and mitigate them so you keep to the rules. Early on you might not have the confidence not to make a special social event a PRD without breaking them – this may be the reality of your situation as it was mine. By not breaking the rules though you'll be doing just fine. All aspects of your being will improve where drink before was addling it including projected lifespan. And you will be properly happy.

CHAPTER SEVEN

MY CONCLUSION – WHAT'S YOURS?

Phew, that was quite a journey for me, now for you. Let me condense down to a few words what has been discussed – how and why one embarks and remains on the path:

You've made the decision that the upsides of drink – which boiled down to its bare bones is its narcotic effect upon your brain which causes an unnatural imbalance of chemicals responsible for promoting joy and inhibiting inhibitions – is now of lesser merit than the downsides. The causes of the downsides are mood degradation caused in part by the body overcompensating in righting the chemical imbalances together with detrimental effects to your organs, central nervous system and musculoskeletal system (in fact there isn't much left of you which isn't affected by chronic alcohol intake). The behavioural effects of these elements vary from person to person – depending on what makes you tick, your health and your life situation. I have used myself as an example of how my altered behaviour nearly ruined me. None of us are perfect and even if we had never drank we would never succeed in every situation. But alcohol has made how we perform in most situations in personal and business life worse and we can say simply that how we show ourselves to ourselves and the outside world has been compromised. Therefore the decision has been made to do something about it. With me the decision had been made some time before I embarked on the path but I couldn't break the cycles. I tried so hard to stop but couldn't. I discounted commercial clinics because the cost was prohibitive. I thought about joining help groups of all varieties but knew really that they would not work with me. I can understand the mutually supportive element of the group going through it together and I am not dissing this approach because it has helped many and will continue to do so. For me, though, to be honest, the fact was my alcoholism was my business and not for a declaration to a room of perfectly well meaning but perfect strangers. I believe what you do by yourself, in your own mind, accepted totally by you on your own terms – sticks. No form of prohibition would have worked with me. As the Roman poet Horace said (probably in a different context but not necessarily), 'If you drive nature out with a pitchfork, she will soon be back'.

So a different route to freedom was devised. This route accepts that there are mines laid along the way that would cause us to revert to the old ways if we are not prepared for them. Stoicism and fortitude are required but are not enough. The Trigger is there, primed ready to strike and scythe through our defences and get us back on the booze. We must create the conditions through which it won't be pulled. If we say never again to drink, a hard stop, it will eventually fire out of the blue and without warning. We know it does because we restarted the cycles many times – just as we thought we were in the clear. This is the realpolitik of the situation. The path gives us our project, a plan where all the factors of what might make us drink regularly and heavily again are identified and mitigated. The central tenet of the strategy is the use of Planned Relapse Days. These provide a buttress against full relapse because all our cravings are deferred to them, taking away our distraction and releasing us to excel. But in order that the PRDs don't become a proxy for your old patterns of drinking there are three Oaken Rules which are there to ensure your drinking reduces toward zero. By following the Oaken Rules and not transgressing the red lines you set for yourself you cannot backslide. Continuous improvement is automated, built in to the strategy. The PRDs allow you to reassess what alcohol is to you, to ring fence all the feelings and experiences it imparts to you and see them for what they are. This is a progressive improvement made possible by successive PRDs. The PRDs become less important to us. Eventually their importance diminishes so much that the need for them may dissipate altogether. We recover thoughtfully and completely on the Recovery Days after each PRD. Every other day becomes a Standard Day on which our improvement continues. In the early days of the path we need to utilise the Creeping Barrage technique to fill days so we have no time for brooding. This is one tactical weapon in an arsenal we have ready to deploy against specific situations and temptations that life will throw up especially during the first strides. Forewarned is forearmed. There are booze imps chattering away on our shoulders, quite loquacious at first and persuasive against which our counter arguments must be sound and instantly ready to deploy. There are social situations that need to be planned for so you don't get caught on the hop. There are tactical weapons that are utterly practical in ensuring you physically don't put booze in your mouth when you're not supposed to. Running concurrently with the alcohol reduction along the path is health improvement. This is a natural effect of drink reduction but also we boost further our improvements in mind and body through exercise and diet – each according to what they can manage. The sum of the whole of the continuous improvement is greater than its parts. The real damage to our health that alcohol can do is avoided. Finally we measure our progress to show ourself how great we are doing by means of simple stats. What a buzz to see those ol' graphs going ever downward. Who knows – as another Roman poet this time Virgil once wrote – 'The day may dawn when this plight shall be sweet to remember'.

Where had I come from? Booze was destroying me no question in mind and body. Healthwise as I have said I could see the symptoms of increasing danger rising. It was as though the very marrow of my bones was crying out the lamentations of the drinking years. Health though is not what made me do something to break the cycles. It was the pervading thought, with me during my thirties, but gaining ever more momentum that I was not fulfilling my potential and years were becoming lost. If it had not been for this I may well have continued until the symptoms became do or die. This is not to say that my health considerations did not significantly add to the need to address my boozing, but it was driven primarily by my desire for a second chance to become the best person I could be. The third element was to do it for the person whose happiness was directly affected by my drinking, my wife. Three forces at work then in the makeup of my decision, each coming to the fore at different times but the need for me myself to cut away the balloon anchor of booze and soar skywards dominant.

When I look back to how detrimental my drinking was, I am saddened but also amazed to realise that up to the point I embarked on the path I wasn't destitute or in jail. At the very least I should have been going everywhere by Shank's pony. I had access to drink from a very young age. My dad made home brewed beer and would keep the finished bottles in a cupboard under the stairs. Starting at fourteen, I used to sneak under and have swigs from each bottle and top up with water so not to arouse suspicion. My drink thievery became a regular occurrence. I was happy to just get the feel of it then stop on any particular night and also not drink enough to have to water it down too much and get found out. But the seed had been sown. Is drinking in the blood? From my experience no – my dad was always very moderate and disciplined in his drinking and would never derelict his duty to his family by causing it to affect his work. But if you have any responsibility for any youngster – please, please do what you can to ensure they do not have any alcohol as a child. It increases the chance significantly of full alcoholism later – I would spare them this. Up to the end of university I treated drink the same as most other kids of that age – getting drunk at parties and making a fool of myself – although at university I did gain a reputation as someone who buys cans every night. In my final year it was undoubtedly the cause that I did not get the grade that was predicted for me the previous year. It was during my first job after graduating that it really took hold. My degree was in Business Management specialising in Supply Chain and I was working as a graduate trainee for a big catalogue company in a real bear pit of a logistics department. Under huge pressure every day to get the parcels out and delivered, my role was as a first line supervisor to a team of drivers. The spotlight was on me to perform because I was on a fast track programme. My shift was 06:00-14:00. It was hard to get a good traineeship at that time and if you did well it would really set up your career. Here's how I set up my career. I would get back to my flat at 14:45. I would go for a run (tick in the box). Then I would buy and drink a 2.5 litre bottle of 8% White Lightening cider. I would smoke three cigarettes with it. Then before just going to bed eat a big meal. I had to wake at 04:30 to get into work on time. The first few hours were very busy as I had to get the drivers on the road in time so had little time to think, just react. But the previous evening's excess crept up on me and I became of less and less use during the day. In that job the supervisors who stayed after hours to prepare thoroughly for the next day were noticed by management. I always left at 14:00 to the second. Over three years I saw the members of my graduate intake promoted while I stayed at the same level. Worse, after consistent poor performance and a reputation amongst all staff that 'I always seemed to have my head in the clouds' I was removed from supervisory duties. I should have been sacked – it was only because of the high turnover of staff at the depot and the need for pairs of hands on deck that I wasn't. I never once thought that my drinking was a problem. Still only in my mid twenties and with my overall optimism for my life undiminished – because it was *them* who had failed me in the job, I put into action a plan I'd had since university to go abroad for a while. I was always very good at planning my next big move. I went to New Zealand for three years. I was lucky enough to be in the right place at the right time to get an internal Supply Chain consulting role with New Zealand freight railways. I loved it and got on very well with my boss who was a great mentor and I wish I could have done him prouder in my subsequent roles. Even though I was happy at work I would still go home at night and drink a couple of bottles of wine. This time the nature of the role though was as close to a perfect fit for me as could be which papered over the negative effects of the drink. Besides, I did exercise and was young enough to take it and show up to the office every day relatively fresh. Career being still the most important thing to me at this time, although I was really having a fine time in NZ I returned to the UK and a new job. I fell into a thirties rut caused by my continued drinking. I would get progressively better and more senior roles – getting jobs wasn't the problem. When I had obtained an interview, I would stop drinking and prepare very effectively for it. So I would beat many other candidates and started the new job with all wanting me to do well which would carry me through the first six probationary months. Then, with preordained inevitability I would after two years or so (this period diminishing with each job) trip over the stalagmite formed by the constant dripping of the drink. What about your personal relationships at this time I hear you ask? You may ask. Not good. Never a confident person around the opposite order, the confidence sucking nature of alcohol meant I didn't think the best of my ability to carry off a long relationship successfully so didn't try very hard. I couldn't see why anyone would be interested in me for the long haul. Although obviously dependant on it, alcohol was still on balance more fun than anguish and not enough time had accumulated for me to start looking back at my life with regret. Dates and relationships were obtained via the new broadsheet dating sites and LinkedIn, which I used as such a site – my profile heading announcing: 'Likes DIY and garden chores – good listener'. A succession of two-month romances were unsuccessfully completed as I saw my university friends marry and have children. The less than roaring forties began. I had a stroke but of luck when I met my wife quite unexpectedly. Best thing to happen to me by light years. I still continued with the same old career pattern though – my wife worked abroad for long periods at this time and during her leave I would relent but start drinking again when she went back. As soon as we'd wed I finally got a mortgage and house and vowed never to ever take drink over its doorstep. The night after I moved in with great ceremony, I bought my last eight cans that would ever be in the house. Three years later I was still hopelessly trapped in the booze cycles and my wife was increasingly worried. I had been off a booze cycle for three days and needed to mend urgently a loose window frame to stop rain coming in. I searched the garage and found a bag of screwdrivers that I hadn't used since I had bought them just after we moved in. I set them down to eat my cereal first. I realised I hadn't in four years really experienced the house. I looked up from my bowl of Frosties and cried sugar tears because all the worlds were yet to conquer. The downsides of drink tipped the scales. My attempts at breaking the drinking cycles were not working. I decided on another path.

That was then, this is now. Two yearsish since I started on the path. Time elapsed though is not the important thing – it is the progress you make and how your personal relationship with booze changes as it tends towards zero in volume and significance that counts. In the past when I'd really tried to give up booze repeatedly breaking the cycles, on paper it looked like I was doing well with drink. During my best efforts the cycles could look like: nineteen days off, three on, nineteen off, two on, nineteen days off, four on. That's not that much drinking. But booze and the thought of it was always dominant – I kept going back to it and The Trigger's barrel was hot. Now I feel immensely better. No bit of me has swelled up due to alcohol since the second PRD. I used only to be able to do the low impact cardio exercises at the gym but have now rediscovered jogging after many years thinking it was impossible to ever do again. I still eat too much ice cream but my weight doesn't yo yo now and is where I want it to be. I never feel my heart fluttering like a Red Admiral (nor yet a Cabbaged White) anymore. I've press-upped my moobs away.

I had always loathed self pity in others but it had been integral to me for such a long time. Alcohol is liquid self pity and I'll tell you if I can point to one of the best outcomes of the path it is how it becomes less and less of a force and is replaced by inner confidence and belief. With setbacks now I look forward thinking how I can do better next time and plan to succeed. With any success I've replaced wallowing in the glow of success with desire to press home the advantage. The way I face out to the outside world is much better and more effective now. I'm still a bit shy but don't retreat to my shell as long or often. I still in many ways view the world the same as a horse does. I like everything to be in its right place as I move through it otherwise I get edgy. But the cult of *them* has been replaced by wanting to deal with people on their merits and trying to understand them better. Blimey, I even *network* now! I always knew that in the corporate world it's not what but who you know but still took the attitude that if someone doesn't want to bother with me, whomsoever it is, I won't with them – bugger em. I need others to get on so I try with those I need now and can handle those who in the past would have bested me without a fight because my confidence was always drained. The corporate world especially contains many mountebanks consumed with naked ambition and sheer front that drives then through. People with backsides their backsides talk out of and theirs also – chattering backsides reflected between two plane mirrors to infinity. But it's not my job here to judge others. Too often *I* was a prize bell-end at work – drunkenness begatting bellendedness. My wife and I are consistently happy now. If I hadn't started on the path we would now be apart. We have rows still but of the stop watching telly and dig me the holes for my new rhododendrons you promised me you great lazy git variety – not the vicious ones I propagated that were booze fuelled.

I carry far less fear around with me now. Beer means fear. I can see how far I've come since the path began – I look like a different person to myself. Sometimes I would like to feel as I was about aged fourteen before booze really made its presence felt – the pure me uncorrupted by that bloody stuff. Then I feel sad because I never can. I wish I could have just one hour now, where in all of my life past I'd never known booze. A nirvana that's sadly unattainable.

To see and feel what the adult me never tainted by it would see and feel – to understand what my natural base flaws are without them ever having been influenced and enhanced by booze. To see what I could have been, the absolute best me – something I'll never know because I've known drink. I feel like I want to make amends now. But I don't want to sound too heavy – life is much lighter now and has become a lot easier and immensely more fun. Time really has slowed down but doesn't hang heavy because I know how to use it. The old five o' clock barrier after which I would be safe really means nothing anymore. I can hardly understand the person to which it did and have removed these eddies in the flow of time. I can enjoy the simple pleasures without something else having to be there. I've always loved astronomy – it was the one thing that transcended drink that I wouldn't need booze to get the most out of even in the throes of a deep booze cycle. When I was about sixteen, and evidently already knowing I was becoming corrupted, I composed this ditty to make sure I acknowledged going stargazing was something special and recited it on each occasion – 'when I see the firmament, to bollocks with false merriment'. Now I don't even have to prep myself at all before going out to see the stars and planets. Ditto other pleasures that were usually booze enhanced or where I needed drink immediately after the experience to intensify the memory – a goshawk rising or the first summer gang of swifts screeching overhead. I look forward to waking in the morning.

I enjoy melancholy again, whether in a scene or in my mood, as I did when a child – as well as the crash, bang, wallop of modern experience. I'm more in tune with how others perceive me. If I wanted to make a real go of it career wise, I realised I needed to be more aware of what those other than close friends and family thought of me through my words and deeds – without having to compromise myself to myself. Was this made possible by drinking much less? – well this gave me leave to take a hard look at myself and consciously adjust my behaviour. I've learnt patience and am not frightened anymore. What has replaced the addiction? Life.

I have another PRD planned. I've deferred it once and may do again but it's there if I want it. During my last PRD, I consumed a third of the units of my first and was more than sated. Both my graphs are heading towards zero. Is there a residue of booze in my psyche still? – of course there is it never totally leaves. John Barleycorn though is ever closer to death. I know, though, that all other things being equal I will live much longer and have the remaining time available to me which I can use, each sunrise a opportunity to be useful now, not one to visit a wasted day in la la land before the next. I'm a regular person – nothing special about me. If I can do it you can. You have the will, the method and the tools. Embark on the path and end those terrible cravings, the periods of hell and the effects of booze on your body. Life will become a lot easier. Become the most effective you, imagination unsullied. See again through unadulterated eyes – Mundus in claritate!

This book is printed on paper from sustainable sources managed under the Forest Stewardship Council (FSC) scheme.

It has been printed in the UK to reduce transportation miles and their impact upon the environment.

For every new title that Matador publishes, we plant a tree to offset CO_2, partnering with the More Trees scheme.

For more about how Matador offsets its environmental impact, see www.troubador.co.uk/about/